# *the*
# VENERABLE
# FLY TYERS

# *the* VENERABLE FLY TYERS

## ADVENTURES IN FISHING AND HUNTING

## Dave Jankowski

MISSION POINT PRESS

The following stories were previously published:
"Thoughts From 35,000 Feet," The Planing Form Newsletter, #64, Jul/Aug 2000
"The Fishwagon," *The Riverwatch,* #78. Summer 2018
"The Fishmaster," *The Riverwatch,* #80, Spring 2019

Readers are encouraged to go to MissionPointPress.com to contact the author or
to find information on how to buy this book in bulk at a discounted rate.
For information or permission, contact:

Mission Point Press
2554 Chandler Road
Traverse City, Michigan 49696
www.MissionPointPress.com

Printed in the United States of America

Cover Art: Winslow Homer (artist) American, 1836–1910

Softcover ISBN: 978-1-954786-69-1
Hardcover ISBN: 978-1-954786-70-7

Library of Congress Control Number: 2022900266

# CONTENTS

INTRODUCTION   *xi*

THE VENERABLE FLY TYERS   *1*

FIRST STEELHEAD   *9*

DEAD DRIFT   *15*

THE FISHWAGON   *21*

MAKING UP CRAP   *27*

THE FISHMASTER   *33*

THE CARP AWARD   *39*

DAN WAS RIGHT   *45*

WIVES, CHILDREN, AND FISHING   *51*

THE RILEY NEWMAN LETTERS   *53*

ZEN AND THE ART OF FLY FISHING   *63*

ODE TO THE LLAMA   *65*

CALL ME DEADEYE   *67*

A FISHING LEGEND AND THE WORLD WIDE WEB   *75*

A FIFTY GRAYLING DAY   *77*

JIMMY BUFFET, IF YOU READ THIS   *83*

THE MOUSE THAT ROARED   *85*

HALF-DAY BUDDY   *93*

THE LAST ROCK IN THE LAMAR   *101*

A THOUSAND-DUCK POTHOLE   *107*

WHAT KIND OF WHISKEY WAS THAT?   *113*

WHY I FISH   *121*

GENESIS   *123*

WHY BAMBOO   *133*

STEFAN SHOT LAST   *139*

SAVING WHISTLE PIG   *147*

ROD'S RODS   *153*

ANOTHER ROCK IN THE LAMAR   *163*

DENNY'S WAKE   *169*

THOUGHTS FROM 35,000 FEET   *173*

THE CABIN   *175*

GRAMPY'S CABIN   *185*

RIVER TIME   *191*


ABOUT THE AUTHOR   *193*

ABOUT THE ARTIST   *194*

GRATITUDE   *195*

*To Mary, who sometimes lets me go fishing,*
*and who always welcomes me home.*

This book is additionally dedicated to the disabled American Veterans who have so honorably served their country since the early days of Vietnam, through all the Mideast conflicts, to this day and beyond. When I address these men and women on the first day of the Bamboo Bend Project, I do not thank them for their service, for I too have served, instead I thank them for their sacrifice. Whether they are physically impaired or suffer from PTSD, it does not matter, they have given up so much of their well-being for the well-being of our nation.

Project Healing Waters Fly Fishing (PHWFF) is a national program dedicated to the healing of these veterans. Through the galaxy of fly fishing activities; fly casting, outdoor trips, fly-tying, and rod building; participating veterans are given the opportunities to experience the kind of adventures and camaraderie that the stories in this book humbly attempt to share.

Begun in 2005 at Walter Reed Army Medical Center to serve wounded military service members returning from combat in Iraq and Afghanistan, today there are more than two hundred local programs serving more than ten thousand veterans. The national program as well as local programs all depend on voluntary contributions. There are only a dozen staff members at PHWFF, all others are strictly volunteers. Eighty-four percent of contributions directly support the veterans. Twenty percent of the proceeds of this book will be donated to PHWFF.

If you are unfamiliar with these programs, please check them out online at:
projecthealingwaters.org
bamboobend.org

# INTRODUCTION

I didn't always have stories, but have always loved them. When I was a young pilot, there was a WSO (wiz OH—short for Weapons System Operator) in my squadron named Terry Murphy.

My God, he was a good storyteller. He held us young officers spell-bound with his tales of flying in Vietnam. He flew out of Udorn Royal Thai Air Force Base, in the 555 (Triple Nickel) Squadron, the premier air-to-air squadron of Steve Ritchie, Jeff Feinstein, and Chuck DeBellevue, aces all. Terry's stories of chasing MIGs in the back seat of John Madden's F-4 Phantom over the skies of Vietnam mesmerized us. He seemed so much more worldly and older in his mid-thirties than we in our early twenties.

As I have gotten older and moved from flying to fly fishing, I found new stories from the writers John Voelker, Gordon Macquarie, Gene Hill, and others. Their fishing and hunting adventures and society of friends thrilled me.

Then one day, I realized that I had some of those same stories and this book is my attempt to tell them.

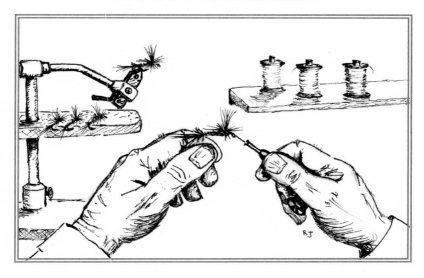

"I think that we should give it to Archer!" exclaimed Doc Scott.

"Yes, let's give it to Archer!" echoed a forum of the Venerable Fly Tyers.

"What … what am I getting?" I stammered.

"Why the Sportsman's Award, of course," said Doc.

"I'm not even a member," I objected.

Doc grinned. "Maybe not, but we always present it here at the annual Christmas party. Your showing us the ropes at Yellowstone this year makes you the natural choice."

A vote was taken, and the next thing I knew, I was standing before the group. Last year's recipient placed a large, framed award in my hands. I examined it closely. Inside the wooden frame, behind glass, was a beautiful, matted picture of two hands carefully releasing a brook trout in full spawning colors. Below the picture, a shadow box cradled a collection of flies, each one masterfully tied by a different member of the Venerable Fly Tyers. Above the picture was a brass plaque that read, *"TO THE MAN WHO DID THE MOST TO PROTECT THE FISH!"*

I was honored and grateful. I thanked last year's recipient, I thanked the president of the Fly Tyers and the vice president, then I thanked the treasurer and the secretary. I thanked each member in turn, then, for good measure, I began thanking their wives.

Before I could complete my solicitous thanking, I heard someone cautiously venture, "Archer is not officially a member … what if he does not return it next year?"

I'd had the award for maybe two minutes, and already somebody was worried that I wouldn't give it back. A discussion followed. Members joined sides and pressed their arguments. My integrity, or lack of it, was discussed. The argument had reached a heated pitch before Viking quieted the mob and said, "I'm a Washtenaw County deputy sheriff. I know where he lives. I could get a squad car and SWAT team over to his house in five minutes. We'll get it back!" With that, the crowd cheered and I got to keep the darn thing.

When I got home later that night, I placed my new treasure on the wall next to the fireplace, in a position of honor. Not only was I proud to receive it, it just looked so darned good hanging there. For the next year, I stopped and admired it every time I walked past. December came, and I received my invitation to the Venerable Fly Tyers' Christmas party. Enclosed was a hand-scrawled note that said, "Don't forget to return the Sportsman's Award!"

Did I have to double-bolt my door, install an expensive alarm system, and peek out of shuttered windows to see if that SWAT team was lurking about? No, I didn't. I had a better idea. They were worried about me returning the award. What if I *didn't* return it? What if I returned something else altogether? So, in my spare time, I started beavering away in my workshop. I constructed a frame that looked just like the one on the Sportsman's Award. I matched the matting and the textured background. I found a picture of a hand holding … well not a brook trout … but a carp; a fat, golden-scaled, bugle-lipped, bottom-feeding carp, and glued it in the center. Then I made a shadow box and filled it with the cast-off dregs of my early fly-tying attempts. One fly had a loose thread hanging down two inches. Another had the hackle completely unwinding. I made a new brass plaque, had it inscribed, and put it above the picture. Finally, I fitted the frame with a glass front and wrapped the whole contraption in brown paper.

On the night of the party, I arrived fashionably late and sashayed around, carrying my package. I was greeted with relief. Hands reached out to be shaken, I was patted on the back, and soon a drink was placed in my hand. I was a hale and hearty fellow. Everyone said that they were glad to see me. They practically shouted in unison, "Hooray! We knew all along that you would bring the Sportsman's Award back!"

I settled into the festive atmosphere. Dishes were shared and liquor flowed freely, ties were loosened, jackets and sweaters removed. Men who normally keep a bit of distance were squeezing shoulders, patting backs, and touching arms as they laughed and boisterously told and retold their stories. Some I had heard at last year's party. Yet somehow they were better this year. The rivers were swifter, the fights were longer, and the fish were bigger!

The wives, dressed in their finest and holding small glasses of the same libations their men were guzzling, huddled in their own corner. They sipped their drinks while watching their men in disbelief. What troglodytes they had married—men who took so much delight in such childish pursuits. I overheard one woman say, "Can you believe it, they even put them back?"

When the storytelling had run its course and bellies were full, Bald Eagle, the president of the Venerable Fly Tyers, called the business portion of the event to order. First, there were elections. Bald Eagle's term as president was extended unanimously. A new vice president was elected, as well as a secretary and treasurer. Next, came the presentation of awards. The "Big Fish" went to Tom's twenty-incher, after the discussion of a valid witness was settled. Rusty, again recognized as the best fly tyer in the group, took the Fly-Tying Award. Then came the Sportsman's Award. After several nominations, more stories, and much discussion, Viking became this year's proud recipient.

I was called forth to present the award. Viking joined me at the podium and we stood together facing the group. I removed the brown paper wrapper and held the award so only he and I could see it. I thanked the group and described the wonderful trophy that was in my hands. I said the fish was beautiful, and that the flies were marvelous examples of craftsmanship and detail. Viking, looking on, could hardly contain himself as I rambled on. His sniggering was about to give me away. Finally, I said I liked the plaque and read it out loud: *"TO THE MAN WHO DID THE MOST TO EN-SURE THE FISH GOT AWAY!"* Viking, in one swift move, seized the award, turned it, and held it high for all to see. The room went dead quiet, eyes glazed, and mouths dropped open. This *was not* the Sportsman's Award! It was something else, something perhaps … even profane. Then the president snickered, chuckled, and finally guffawed. Following his lead, all laughed. Even the wives laughed.

The fake was passed around for everyone to see, eliciting much comment and more laughter. However, it wasn't long before an armed escort took me out into the cold night to retrieve the "real" Sportsman's Award from the trunk of my car. That restored, I was the man of the moment. It was decided, by unanimous vote, that I should become a member. I accepted with feigned humility.

Then, the question arose, "What do we do with the carp picture?" The president said, "Let's give another annual award, 'to the man who did the most to ensure the fish got away'—to the biggest screwup of the year!"

When I joined the Venerable Fly Tyers that night, the group had been together for over twenty years—a dozen men, from all walks of life, with one thing in common: the love of fly fishing and fly-tying … or is that two things?

Several members had been there from the beginning, from that first get-together of a few fishing buddies and the idea that "We should meet regularly, tie flies, drink beer, and tell stories. Yes, let's do that!"

In the months and years that followed, members were added, new fishing buddies and fly tyers met along the way. Others left the group when promotions or new jobs took them to places far away. Marriages broke up and kids grew up. The joys and sorrows of life were easily shared with the members of the Venerable Fly Tyers.

By the time I became a member, the group's routine was set. They met twice a month, alternated homes, and served snacks and brew. And, of course they tied flies. Two of the members had taught fly-tying for local fly shops and had elevated the craft to an art form. Others tied serviceable flies for their own fishing needs. I was the only beginner and considered it my great fortune to be part of this group.

My introduction to the Venerable Fly Tyers had been none other than the president himself, Rod Jenkins. Rod and I flew together for Northwest Airlines and had met at the Portland Air National Guard on a drill weekend.

Rod was in the unit, flying F-101s, and I was trying to "get in," peddling my F-4 background. My bid to join the squadron was unsuccessful, but a more important thing happened: I became friends with Rod Jenkins.

Rod was tall and lean then, hair light and already sparse. He had an easy manner and a ready smile. We were of the same age and shared a similar background as fighter pilots: He, of course, with the Oregon Guard and F-101s, I with the Air Force and eventually the Michigan Guard and F-4s. And we had our airline jobs. We never actually flew together at Northwest because we were too close in seniority, so our careers paralleled in aircraft and positions. We were first officers and later captains at the same time.

Our friendship blossomed when we each moved to the Detroit area and discovered that we both were fly fishing fanatics. He'd been doing it since childhood, and I was relatively new at the game. Although he didn't introduce me to fly fishing (Ducker did that), he quickly became my mentor and we began to take fishing trips together.

Although I usually called him Rod, the Venerable Fly Tyers referred to him in more formal terms. To them he was either the "President" or the "Fishmaster." Although he would earn the title "Fishmaster" over and over again on every outing, it was not the name that he chose to call himself. That was "Bald Eagle," a reflection (pun intended) on the hairlessness of his large, size-eight head. Not a name really, but more of a "tactical call sign" from the tradition of flying fighter aircraft.

A tactical call sign is your very own, original call sign that is used on all your flights. It is actually registered and cannot be duplicated. The idea behind it was that in the heat of battle you responded quicker to a familiar name than to the unit sign and number of the old system. The Navy had used familiar names for years. We all remember "Maverick" and "Goose" from the movie *Top Gun*, but do we remember the characters' given names … Pete Mitchell and Nick Bradshaw? After the huge recruiting success of that movie, the Air Force decided that they couldn't miss out on a good opportunity like that, so we were all tasked to select our own call signs.

Mine was "Archer," a name I chose myself to avoid getting labeled "Gyro" after my near miss with Lake Huron during a spatial disorientation incident. Tactical call signs given by your squadron mates can be cruel. Some I have known include "Throwback," "Toe Jam," and "Vomit." I have to admit, Archer isn't anything particularly clever. I took a dictionary, started with the As and never got out of them. By the time I found Archer, I was tired of the whole drill, and besides, it had a warrior ring to it and sounded like someone who could shoot. Had I gotten tired earlier, I might have been "Aardvark." Anyway, I could say "Archer" in public and wear it proudly on my chest, and so it stuck.

Many tactical call signs go with the pilot's last name. For instance: "Alka" (Smeltzer), "Cabbage" (Patch), or "Notso" (Smart). Another, "Scratch," for my friend Rich Tomich, is because he has so many itches in his name. Others like "Ayatollah," "Gunner," and "Pyro," reflect the pilot's character. "Bramage" for Dane White—need help—brain damage—Dane Bramage. You get the idea!

My all-time favorite is "Moses." As the story goes, this intrepid aviator was flying an F-4 Phantom carrying a two-thousand-pound shape, an inert cement training bomb. In flight, he had an inadvertent release—that is, the shape came off the airplane prior to arrival at the bombing range. It fell into a small lake. As it "divided the water," it nearly killed a guy in a rowboat. After he cleaned his pants, this hapless bait fisherman had a heyday picking up all the fish that had washed ashore. "More effective than dynamite," he was heard to mutter. "Hey, Moses, you going to fish or cut bait?"

So, the Venerable Fly Tyers, emulating their leader, quickly picked up the tradition. Gary Moyski became Mathman or simply Moyski. Craig Swenson became Viking, Dr. Rick Scott is now Doc, Dave Hellman dropped the Dave and is just Hellman, Dan Flick is Ducker, and Rod Rebant became Whistle Pig, in honor of a bottle of whiskey by that name that he brought to a meeting. In addition to being just plain fun, tactical call signs worked well when we spread out on group fishing trips and maintained contact with handheld radios. "Bald Eagle to Archer … I need a witness for my twenty-inch fish!"

It should be no surprise that Bald Eagle and I were attracted to fly fishing after flying jet fighters. Both are multidiscipline sports. In flying, you need a working knowledge of aerodynamics, electrics, hydraulics, mechanics, jet propulsion, navigation, and meteorology. Fly fishing depends on your understanding of fish, insects, stream dynamics, water hydrology, casting, and

… meteorology! They both require fine-tuned and practiced hand-eye coordination. They depend on the vehicle that takes you there, the aircraft and the fly rod. And a love for these vehicles quickly develops. They are highly visual. They require special equipment: a flight suit, helmet, g-suit, and gloves versus waders, Tilley hat, vest, and … gloves. And finally, they both are dangerous: You can get into trouble in the blink of an eye!

In fact, I love everything to do with flying and fly fishing. Perhaps Richard Bach said it best in his book *Stranger to the Ground*: "When you truly love something, you love performing even its most mundane tasks." I love handling the equipment, tying on a new tippet, and cleaning the rod and line before the next day on the stream. I love opening my fly box and selecting a fly—and I love tying that fly!

I wasn't always a fly tyer, but I have always been a maker of things. As a young boy, I learned to sew, make puppets, kites, and crude wooden projects in my father's workshop. My wife once asked me why I had so many different hobbies. I answered, "No, dear, I only have two. I like making things and I like being outdoors." Fly fishing and its constellation of activities are the perfect confluence of the two.

It didn't take many fishing trips for me to realize that buying all the flies I needed at two dollars a whack would get expensive. So, it occurred to me that tying my own flies would save a fortune. That soon proved to be folly as my collection of hooks, thread, tinsel, chenille, dubbing, feathers, fur, and tools grew to fill several bins and occupy an entire corner of my den. It was not cheaper, but it was so much more fun!

I started fly-tying with a book and a cheap kit that I picked up for three dollars at a garage sale. The book was Richard Talleur's *The Fly Tyer's Primer*, and to him I forever owe my gratitude. Under Talleur's guidance, I learned on the road during my airline trips. I spent countless hours in motel rooms putting otherwise idle time to good use by learning fly-tying. I often wondered what the maids must have thought, "Who killed the chicken and the squirrel in this room?"

After about three months, I had tied every fly in Talleur's book and had updated the kit with many new materials, tools, and a better vise. I began to see the world as a materials warehouse. I stopped for every road-killed pelt I could find, and with the help of Eric Leiser's *Fly-Tying Materials*, I preserved them. This habit was not popular with my family. Driving my daughters to after-school lessons one day, I stopped for a freshly killed groundhog. When I got back in the car, I found both girls hiding on the floor. They wailed, "Dad, everyone will think that we're so poor that we have to eat these things!"

Eventually my local fly shop offered a class on tying, so I signed up. Although I learned little new, the class did validate what I had learned from Talleur's book. I was ready, set, and dangerous. It was at that time that I was admitted to the ranks of the Venerable Fly Tyers.

# FIRST STEELHEAD

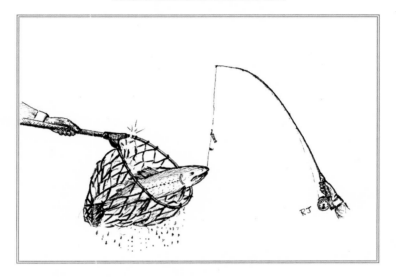

"Look at that guy!" said Ducker with a sneer.

"What about him?" I asked.

"He's got three thousand dollars' worth of gear on—that's what!"

"How can you tell?"

"I've seen expensive gear before; he looks like a walking Orvis store. I'll bet he's from Chicago too—Ontario Street!"

As we got closer, sure enough, I could see little Orvis tags on everything: the rod, reel, vest—even his hat said Orvis.

Now don't get me wrong—I have nothing against Orvis. They make fine fishing equipment and outdoor clothing, and today I proudly own some of their gear. But, at that time in my life, I couldn't afford their stuff. In fact, there I was walking upstream in old, leaky Red Ball rubber waders. Underneath I wore Air Force issue long underwear from my tour in Iceland. I carried a fly rod and reel that I bought at a discount store. I had an old metal fly box with a mere half dozen flies that Ducker had tied and a ten-dollar pair of Polaroid sunglasses.

Ducker wouldn't let it go. "He's in the best hole, too! We'll just have to go around him and fish the run above. Hell, we'll be lucky to even see a fish!"

"Oh well," he continued, "it's too late in the season anyway—late

April—we should have been here a month ago. The Pere Marquette just doesn't fish well this late."

"At least it's a nice day," I offered, "sunny and warm."

"You don't know anything about steelhead fishing, do you, Archer?"

I guess I didn't. Ducker had me there for the first time just the year before. I didn't even own a fly rod then and had to use an old spinning rod. But I was better prepared this year. After that trip last year, I bought a forty-dollar Berkley fly rod from my local Kmart. I practiced all summer on bluegill and bass in my backyard pond. I learned to throw a passable loop and occasionally even caught a fish.

Ducker and I continued to walk upstream along the old fisherman's trail. Other fishermen we passed reported neither seeing nor taking any fish. Reasons varied: "too late in the season," "the sun was too high," or "the water too clear." It was all stacking up to be the same as last year—we would not catch any steelhead.

As we approached the run above Orvis's hole, we scanned the gravel through our Polaroids and confirmed the reports—no fish! But we were there, so we might as well settle in and fish. What else could we do—go home? Not on your life—there were chores to do there. Besides, Ducker and I always seemed to make the best out of what looked like a poor situation. We did it time and again with poor draws while duck hunting at Harsens Island; we'd end up with a spot no one else wanted and make a banner day at it.

Ducker put me on a good hole behind an old redd and moved further upstream. I cast my fly into the dark water in the shade of a leaning cedar. That tree had leaned that way for a long time; you could tell by the old trunk that lay in the water and the new trunk with branches reaching straight up for the sun. It reminded me of the old willow on my grandfather's lake property in Wisconsin, where I grew up. It hung so far out over the water that we could dive from its limbs. Fish hung out under it, and I caught my first rock bass and bluegills while perched on its almost horizontal trunk. Directly under the trunk, on the bottom, was an old log. My father said that old log was once the trunk that he fished from as a kid. He said the tree was like a wheel revolving into the water with every generation.

There was nothing fancy about my fishing for steelhead on the Pere Marquette that day. It was chuck-and-duck fly fishing with a heavy slinky drifter and big bright egg flies, spring wigglers, and PM caddis. With about twenty feet of line beyond the rod tip, I'd toss the rig up and across the stream. When the slinky made contact with the bottom, I felt its tick-tick-tick as it rolled down the gravel towards me. I followed the downward progress of the drift until line tension and current lifted my rig off the bottom and swung it towards the center of the stream. Then, with a water load, I tossed it back up and did it all over again. The repetitive, mechanical motion encouraged my mind to wander until it settled into the flow of the river, the beauty of the day, and the good feeling of being alive. And there, always somewhere in the background, was the hope of a big fish.

I don't know how long I stood there or how many casts I made. I do know that the sun had been high in the sky when I started and now was closing in on the ridge above. Time had become meaningless and was washed away in the drift of the river and the cast.

And then something changed. It was ever so subtle, but the drift had stopped early, directly under the cedar. I tightened the rod a bit to make contact with the fly. I can hardly describe what happened next: a hard head-shake and then what looked like three feet of chrome and steel shot up out of the water higher than my head. It hung at the top, like Michael Jordan leaping to dunk, and seemed to linger in the air. Then slowly the fish rotated—I swear it looked at me—and fell back into the water with purpose. I had been so deep in my reverie and so shocked by all this, that I took two backward half steps before regaining my balance.

A steelhead is the wildest of creatures. It is not like a salmon that runs up a river but once in its lifetime, to spawn and die. No, once a steelhead gets the taste of the spawning run, it comes back every year, fulfills its primal urges, and then returns to the freedom of the big lake. In the river, it loves the feel of fast-flowing currents yet is confined by stream banks and shallow water. Hook a steelhead and you have hooked into pure, surging energy. The bite of the hook in its mouth makes it go berserk. Its first reaction, more often than not, is a sudden, powerful, water-spraying leap into the air, quickly followed by a hard downstream run. You need to go after it and hope you are in shallow enough water so that you can lift your feet and run with it. It'll often stop in the first big pool; then it is in and out of the water again and again. And, if you don't point your rod right at it when it leaps, you'll lose it. You can count on at least one run right at you. You hope that it is well hooked because you can't strip line fast enough to maintain tension. And, as soon as you have a pile of line at your feet, it is off to the races again. With any luck, it will be upstream this time. If hooking into a salmon is like hooking into a freight train, a hooked steelhead is a jet fighter—an F-16 of tight turns and afterburner, using the vertical every chance it gets.

At that time, I knew nothing about fighting a large fish and soon was plowing through thigh deep water following it downstream. My reel sang like an opera soprano, and soon I was well into my backing. Instinctively, I knew not to pressure the fish when I had so much line in the strong current. I just tried to catch up, regaining line as I could. In all, it must have run four hundred yards. As it approached the deep hole in the bend below, I tried to put the brakes on. Disaster loomed; I knew the hole was full of debris. Ducker, aware of my situation, crossed the stream behind me and ran down the far bank hoping to borrow a net. He found one with Mr. Orvis and got in the stream just below the fish, in the shallow water above the hole. The fish still had plenty of life and wouldn't let Ducker get close with the net. But at least Ducker was pushing it upstream and away from danger.

Time and a good hookset were on my side and eventually the fish began to tire. Ducker had it in and out of the net twice. On his third attempt, he broke the tippet with the net. Just as I thought it was all over and the fish free, Ducker lunged head first, arms and net outstretched, and, with a belly flop, clapped down on the tired fish, pinning it to the bottom in the shallow water. Deliberately, Ducker came to his knees and deftly rolled the net with the steelhead in it. Then he stood, dripping wet, and smiling from ear to ear. A grinning Mr. Orvis helped him up onto the bank.

My relief was palpable as I had thought the fish lost. Now, anxious to catch up with Orvis and Ducker, I reeled my line and hurried downstream. As I neared the pair, Ducker was returning the now-bent metal net. But Orvis apparently didn't care; his attention was on the great fish that lay at his feet. It had been my fish but now belonged to all three. Each of us had taken part.

As I approached my two good comrades, Orvis glanced at me and then my fly rod. He must have seen something familiar in it, for he shouted excitedly, "Is that an Orvis rod?"

"Hell no," I replied … "Kmart!"

# DEAD DRIFT

Aheavy mid-winter snow falls outside my window. Flakes as big as duck eggs swirl in and out of the light from the corner lamppost. I sit in my easy chair with a blanket across my lap; it is early and the furnace hasn't ramped up yet. Coffee is brewing and will be ready soon; its delicious smell already has me wanting. Mary snoozes, still in the warm bed that I left minutes ago. She'll sleep another two hours, until I wake her. In the meantime, I revel in the quiet morning.

I look across the den at my fly-tying desk. There are dozens of books, boxes of material, and whole animal pelts and bird skins hanging on the wall. There are some twenty fly boxes filled with flies that I had spent hundreds of hours tying. So much stuff all related to fly fishing, but none of it fly fishing itself. The sheer weight of this stuff makes me, for a moment, wonder if I have ever actually fished. I am like the man who dreamed he was a butterfly, then awoke and wondered, is he a man who dreamed of being a butterfly or was he a butterfly dreaming he is a man?

What is the essential nature of fly fishing? For me, it is a fish coming out of apparently nowhere to take your tethered and drifting fly, pull it under, and come taut on the end of your line. You have a brief struggle with the fish, bring it to net, then to hand, gaze at its shimmering beauty, then let it slip back into the stream. Its gills flare, taking oxygen from the water. We air-breathing mortals can only wonder at what that is like ... yet envy the freedom a fish has in its watery world. But the very essence of the whole experience was that moment the fish took the fly. All before was preparation, all after consequence. A moment so fleeting and ephemeral, that as I sit here, I wonder if it had ever happened. In mid-winter, I often wonder if I have ever fished!

Fly fishing in the aggregate is so much, yet in its essence so simple. I am reminded that I need to spend more time on the water. But it won't happen today; the winter season holds me prisoner in my own house. Today I can only do the accessory things, one of which is to sit and remember.

As I return my gaze to my fly-tying desk, my eyes settle on a book, one book out of dozens on the shelf, the book that started this whole, wonderful obsession. And I remember another day in another season when I had just begun fly fishing ....

I looked out the window on a bright July morning. The heat of the day hadn't come yet, but it loomed. A light breeze riffled through the leaves of the sugar maples in my front yard; a cloud of midges danced in a ray of sunlight. My thoughts turned to how I would spend this fine day. I thought of a television show that I saw once: Grandpa Walton visited his country cousin. Grandpa Walton wasn't exactly a city slicker himself, but the cousin lived so far in the backwoods that even Grandpa couldn't imagine how he spent his time. He queried his cousin and got this reply: "When I get up in mornin', I ask myself, 'Should I hunt, fish, or make whiskey?'"

As I pondered those three excellent choices, a vehicle turned in to my driveway. It was Ducker's Bronco. Ducker didn't usually show up unannounced, so I wondered what he wanted. Did I have something of his? Was he returning something of mine? Did he need to borrow money or share a good story? I wondered if he knew about Grandpa Walton and his cousin!

I watched him smartly pop out of his car. He took a couple of quick steps, then abruptly stopped and looked at the front door, then turned his head and looked at the back door. He stood there, wavering like a cattail in the wind. Decisions trouble Ducker. He could always see the advantages to either course of action, and he knew well that choosing one eliminated the other. Then he smiled his little thin-lipped smile and decided on the front door. He had a package in his right hand and carried it with determination and purpose. Other than his dalliance with decisions, Ducker wasn't one to waste time.

I stayed out of sight and let him knock on the door, then quickly opened it wide and let out a "Ho!"

He startled, fell back a step, but quickly recovered. Then he reached forward with the package in his outstretched arms, and said simply, "Here. This is for you, Archer. Read it!"

As I took the package, I offered, "Come on in … coffee?"

"I can't," he said. "I have a lot to do."

"Are you going to hunt, fish, or make whiskey?" I asked.

"What are you talking about?" I guess he didn't know about Grandpa Walton's cousin.

As he sped away, I opened the package. It was a book, large format and hardbound, used, but in good shape. The title was *Mayflies, the Angler, and the Trout* by Fred Arbona. The title seemed silly. I skimmed through it and couldn't believe how much detail the author obsessed about something as small and insignificant as a mayfly. There were so many kinds, and he took up each one with complete thoroughness. In the center of the book were colored plates of all the species that he described. These pictures all looked like the same bug to me. Like mug shots, they all looked identical, unshaven, scowling, and guilty.

Does Ducker really think I'm going to read this, I wondered?

Ducker had introduced me to fly fishing. It was on steelhead that he got me started and it was a steelhead that I first caught on a fly rod. Bass and bluegill were closer to hand. So close, in fact, that they were in my back-yard pond. I improved my skills on them. Don't get me wrong! Bass are fine fish, but they are brutes, generalists that recklessly take anything that looks half-alive. Their appetites are insatiable—you can tell just by the size of their mouths. Thumb-lip even a moderate-sized one and look down its throat—you could stick your fist down there. Trout, on the other hand, are sophisticates that delicately sip only what fancies them at the moment. Oh, the big trout can be brutes, but only occasionally and only after dark, when the rules of stream decorum change.

Ducker knew that I was anxious to try for trout and so intended to set the hook with the gift of this book. Out of courtesy to him, I began to read it from the beginning. As Mr. Arbona described the progression of mayfly species through the season, I marveled at how there always seemed to be something available for the fish to eat. It was as if nature provided a constant conveyer of food to the trout … as if the Divine created trout and then created a way to feed them. He surely must have loved them because he gave them such abundance and variety. This concept had me hooked. It was compelling; it was poetic; and I devoured the rest of the book. Any serious attempt at fly fishing for trout was going to have to go through mayflies!

So captivated was I, in fact, that I headed to my local public library for more books on trout and insects. I checked out several, as well as a video entitled *Anatomy of a Trout Stream*. The video proved to be the ticket, telling me where fish lurked in the stream, flies to catch them, and the importance of presenting those flies with a "dead drift," whatever that was! I watched the video again and still couldn't understand what a dead drift was. Do fish prefer their insects to be dead? Wasn't the fly, made of feather and hair, already dead? What did I have to do to make it more dead? I just didn't get it!

My first trout fishing expedition was to the fabled South Branch of the Au Sable River, some fourteen miles of stream that automaker George Mason bequeathed to the people of Michigan in "perpetuity." I like that word; I think it means forever! His will provided that it remain wild and free of "improvements." Mason knew that a wild trout stream *could not* be improved and wanted to make sure that some Lansing bureaucrat didn't mess with it. The only campground in the tract bore the poetic name of "Canoe Harbor." For five dollars a night, you got a campsite with picnic table and a fire pit. There was a water pump and shared toilets nearby.

When I arrived, it was late July and the campground was almost empty, so I chose the site closest to the river. I deposited my money in the drop box and filled out and posted the permit. Setting up camp could wait; I was eager to fish. I donned my waders and vest and, with fly rod in hand, marched downhill to the stream.

Despite *Anatomy of a Trout Stream*, or perhaps because of it, I wasn't prepared for what I found. The South Branch looked more like a flowing,
melted chocolate bar than a trout stream. I had heard that this branch was
stained with tannin from its boggy upstream source. But I didn't expect this!
The water was so dark and high that it seemed unfishable. How were the fish
going to see my fly, even if I could accomplish the elusive dead drift?

I picked what looked like a shallow spot, and as I eased into the water,
I was quickly up to within an inch of the top of my Red Ball rubber waders.
From the start, wading was a challenge. Every step had to be carefully considered and executed—move a foot forward, feel it touch, shift your weight,
and move the next foot. It was slow going. If I got out into the current at
all, I had to immediately scurry back or get washed away. I fished all day
like that, a good portion of it on my tiptoes, always within an inch or two
of disaster. Although I occasionally drew a bit of water, for the most part I
managed to stay dry.

Wading was a challenge, but casting was even worse. I wasn't a good
caster to begin with, so the added difficulties of high water and staying close
to the bank made it extra challenging. Roll casting was the only option. I
couldn't achieve any distance or accuracy and soon the trees and grass ate
most of my flies. Again, that dead drift, whatever that was … hell, most of
the time, I was just lucky to get the fly out on the water in front of me. My
efforts brought no fish to the surface and no fish rose anywhere else that I
could see.

By the day's end, my limited supply of flies met my limited casting skill,
and I was down to just one fly. I carefully took it out of my fly box and held
it in my left hand. Then with my fly rod gripped in my teeth and elbows
raised in the chest-deep water, I attempted to thread the end of a very short
leader (I didn't know about tippet yet) into the eye of the hook. Then … I
dropped the fly. I reached for it but couldn't quite catch it and watched as
my last hope drifted away. It went just another six inches, and then a fish
rose and took it almost off my fingertips. Then it dawned on me—that was
a dead drift!

I know now how to achieve a dead drift with the fly actually attached to
my line and tippet. I have caught many fish, more than I deserve perhaps,
in that fashion. And I now know better than to fish a blown-out river. But

I doubt that I will ever again feel, as I did on that day long ago, as intimate with a trout stream or as close to a fish as I did the one that took my dead drift!

# THE FISHWAGON

"How much did this baby cost?" asked Bald Eagle.

"One hundred dollars," I answered.

"You got this slide-in camper for a hundred dollars?"

"You bet I did!" I said proudly.

"How much did you pay for the pickup truck?" he asked next.

"Only fifteen thousand dollars."

"That figures, one hundred dollars for the camper and fifteen thousand dollars for the truck to carry the hundred-dollar camper. Sounds like airline pilot economics to me."

"That's a sore subject. We're on strike, you know!" I reminded him.

"Yeah I know, and what better thing to do right now than go fishing in a beat-up fishwagon! Not only are we broke—we look broke!"

And so began the first fishing trip in my "new" camper, also known as the "Fishwagon." My fishwagon was born in Des Moines, Iowa, in 1962, at the factory of Gary's Campers. It was purchased later that year by Bob and Virginia Henk. For many years, they used it to transport their kids around the Midwest on camping and fishing trips. As the kids grew up, it got used less and less until it became a permanent fixture at the end of their driveway.

It had been sitting there in general disrepair, like a lawn ornament gone bad, and used only as a storage site for yard tools.

It came to my attention this way: My wife, Mary, had a small window-treatment business. One day we replaced the verticals on the Henks' sliding glass doors. After the job, I was carrying the empty boxes out of the house, when I noticed the camper and did a double take. Bob must have caught my look because he asked if I would like to see inside it. The next thing I knew, I was standing in a small house, one that would fit inside the four-by-eight-foot bed of a pickup truck. It was furnished with two beds, one over the cab and one that converted into a booth and table. There was a sink with running water, an icebox, stove with gas burners, cupboards, a closet, bin storage, lights—the works. It was as opulent as a sheik's tent. And best of all, it was ready to roll. If there had been an eighth wonder of the world, this would have been it.

I stepped down from this home on wheels and considered the possibilities: no more sleeping on the hard ground, trying to start a fire with wet wood, or drying out waders in the rain. No, this was pure rolling comfort. Just then, Mary stepped out of the house, took one look at me, and in a flash appraised the entire situation. Then she said what I hadn't even thought yet, "You're not bringing that thing home, Dave!"

Not bring it home … yes, that is exactly what I would do. Fishing season wouldn't start until the end of April. I had all winter to whittle away at her resolve.

And so began the winter of my persuasion. Over the course of the next four months, I laid a campaign of obsequiousness, chicanery, and downright deception that would have made an intelligence agency proud. In short, I planted the seeds of my lifetime's greatest acquisition.

"Honey, fishing would sure be more fun if I didn't have to sleep on the ground." "I could even keep a fish or two and bring them home for you if I had an icebox." "If I had a closet, my clothes wouldn't be so wet and dirty when I bring them home." "Honey, that camper would sure make things easier for you."

"Give it up Dave; you're not bringing that thing home!"

And then, a moment of brilliance, the kind that only happens once or twice in a lifetime: "Honey, what if I didn't bring it home? What if I just stored it someplace else?"

"You don't even have a truck," she objected.

"Small detail," I said.

And then, in a rare moment of weakness, she said, "Okay, we do need another vehicle with Kristen driving and all of her school activities. I suppose …." Before she could even begin to reconsider, I was out the door, looking for a truck.

Later, at the wheel of my new previously owned truck, I drove into Bob's driveway. When he came out to meet me, I asked, "Bob, do you remember last fall when you said you wanted two hundred dollars for the camper?"

"Dave, I couldn't sell it to you for two hundred dollars," he replied.

"You … you couldn't?" I stammered.

"No, you're my neighbor. You can have it for one hundred dollars."

With my heart firmly back in my chest, I said, "That is very generous." And, with growing confidence, "Bob, I was prepared to pay two hundred dollars for the camper, so, what if I paid one hundred dollars for it and a hundred more for you to continue to store it in your driveway for a year?"

"It's a deal," he said and led me inside to write up a little contract on his computer … pretty official for a hundred-dollar camper.

I would later find out what a tongue-lashing he received from Virginia for selling the camper and having it still sitting in the driveway. "What was the purpose of selling the camper after all?" she said. "TO GET RID OF IT!"

The next month found me in Bob's driveway, fixing up my new possession. I power washed the exterior and scrubbed and shined the sink. I polished the wood trim with lemon oil, scrubbed the upholstery clean, and laid down new carpet on the floor. I replaced a worn mattress with a new, harder, foam one. I made two wooden wader racks and hung them outside on each side of the door. Mary even made curtains out of duck print fabric. All the while I worked, Virginia watched out her kitchen window, shaking her head and mumbling into the sink. I wondered if she regretted selling it … I wondered if she regretted marrying Bob.

A month later, Bald Eagle and I were headed north. We stopped and camped at the Jackson Hole campsite on the North Branch of the Au Sable River.

What a wonderful trip we had. Caught fish, ate like kings, and slept like babies surrounded by all the comforts of home. When it rained hard one night, we stayed dry in comfortable beds and fell asleep to the rhythm of rain on the metal roof of the Fishwagon.

The next morning, I prepared a sumptuous breakfast, cooking bacon, eggs, and pancakes on the gas burners of the Fishwagon's kitchen. In a particularly gracious mood, Bald Eagle said, "Archer, you know that this fishwagon is probably the best hundred dollars you've ever spent."

"I know," I said. "It is working out so well that I was thinking that maybe I should upgrade. Imagine what I could get for five hundred or even a thousand dollars."

He thought for a moment, then asked, "What would a thousand-dollar camper have that this one doesn't?"

"Well, nothing, but it sure would look better," I said.

"You know, when we leave this fishwagon and go to the stream to fish all day, we leave a lot of expensive gear behind. The way I see it, if you had a nice-looking fishwagon, someone might break into it and steal all our stuff. The way this one looks, they'd be afraid to break in and come face-to-face with some ten-pound rat."

Later, after the day's fishing, we returned to find everything just as we had left it, just as Bald Eagle had predicted. We put our rods and reels away, opened a couple of beers that had cooled all day in the Fishwagon's icebox, and sat under the big oak at the edge of our campsite.

"You know, I've been thinking," Bald Eagle said. He'd fallen into a pensive mood. "When I die, I want to be cremated and have my friends spread my ashes."

"Do you have someplace special in mind?" I asked.

"Not one. Three. I want Patty and the kids to spread a third of my ashes on Mt. Bachelor, where we made all of those Oregon summer hiking outings and winter ski trips. I want Viking to spread a third of them at the Second Meadow of Slough Creek, where we caught so many big cutthroat over the years. And, I want you to spread the last third here on the North Branch, in memory of all our Au Sable fishing trips."

I felt honored to be included in his ash-spreading marathon, and said, "I'll do that, because then you'll be near me when I am dead."

"You want your ashes spread here, too?" he asked.

"No, I want you to rent a backhoe and dig a large hole right here under this big oak. Then, I want you to drive my fifteen-thousand-dollar pickup truck with the hundred-dollar camper, duck curtains and all, into the hole. I want to be laid out on the upper bunk with my waders and fishing vest on. Place my best fly rod ... you know the one I call the Phantom ... in my hand. Set my fly boxes, that cherry net I got last Christmas, and my tying kit around me. Then with the backhoe, fill in the hole. Don't mark the spot. Ten thousand years from now, I want some future archeologist to stumble onto this site. I want him to find the Fishwagon and me, and think, 'This must have been a king to have been so surrounded by riches.'"

"He'll be right," said my friend, "and I'll do it!"

# MAKING UP CRAP

It started with a birthday card that I sent to Bald Eagle. On the front, a man and woman, dressed to the nines, sat across from each other at a small table in a swank restaurant. The man raised a glass of wine and said, "This is the red kind. You can tell by the redness." On the inside of the card, it said, "Another year closer to Making Up Crap."

When Bald Eagle's wife saw it, she said, "That's you Rod, that's what you do all the time. This is the perfect card for you. Who sent it?"

"Archer."

"He does it all the time, too. Why, you two should just send this back and forth on each other's birthdays. You'll never have to buy another card!"

When Bald Eagle and I next met, it was at the Gates Au Sable Lodge. Dining with other members of the Venerable Fly Tyers, we caught up on the twists and turns of our lives since we were last together. The conversation turned to catching fish; the relationship between trout and mayfly; who made better cane rods, Paul Young or Lyle Dickerson; and how soon our wives might let us go fishing again. The subject of the Native American tribes that once roamed Michigan came up. Bald Eagle and I recalled flying at the airlines with a full-blooded Chippewa named Ray Dahl. Ray was six-feet-four-inches tall with wide shoulders and narrow hips. He had a handsome, strong-featured face and wore his jet-black hair down on his shoulders—well beyond airline regulation. He possessed a strength of character and physicality that would have been intimidating but for his ready smile. When I last flew with Ray, he was nearing retirement. His hair was white as snow then and still down on his shoulders—I suppose no chief-pilot had ever had the courage to tell Ray to cut it.

As I related my story, I made a mistake. I did what we all too commonly do; I made a sweeping judgment based on a sample of one. I said, "Ray was from the Chippewa Tribe, you know, the peaceful Indians." I no more than got that out of my mouth before Marvin Roberson, a noted conservationist, jumped up from his nearby table, stalked over, and hovered above me, declaring, "I work with the tribes all the time, and I am here to tell you that the Chippewa were not peaceful. Ask any of the other tribes in the area!" As quickly as he came, he retreated back to his table, satisfied to have slammed the lid on bullshit in the Hungry Fisherman Restaurant.

My buddies looked at me for a long time before I weakly muttered, "Aw heck, Ray was peaceful."

Then Bald Eagle chortled, "Not only were you 'making up crap,' Archer, you got caught 'making up crap!'"

Know that "making up crap" is different than exaggerating the number or length of fish you caught. No, no, "making up crap" requires much more skill than that. It is about telling a good fish story, a skill that, like good wine or cheese, gets better with age. When I was young, I could never tell a good story, because then I had command of the facts. It takes a faltering memory, desperate to express itself, to fill in a few gaps here and there. That's all it is, a little filling in—skillfully done, of course—adding a bit for content, a bit more for clarity, and a bit just to make it interesting. Trying to give a feel for the way it was—to put you there. Never covering up anyone's blunders, oh no, for those make great stories.

Over time the Venerable Fly Tyers have taken to making up crap as an honorable art form. Although we try to outdo each other in the pursuit of "art," the undisputed master of making up crap is Doc Scott. This laconic, self-effacing maven of field and stream can spin a yarn with the best of them. Because he makes little attempt to separate fact from fancy, they become indistinguishable even to those who were there. His presentation is further enhanced as he speaks in such a quiet, unemotional voice that you have to lean in close to hear him.

The Venerable Fly Tyers' Holiday Party is often the scene of such stories. After a couple of Doc's fables, Bald Eagle could no longer restrain himself. He took to the floor of his own living room, and with wild gesticulations and beverage spillage, he turned the table on Doc with this story.

"Doc is a night fisherman. He knows that *Salmo trutta giganteus*, aka the biggest, baddest brown trout in the river, roams the night, looking for easy meals. Course he didn't get big by stupidly wandering about in broad daylight, getting eaten by kingfishers, eagles, osprey, herons, otters, mink, water snakes, or caught by fair-weather, mid-afternoon fishermen.

"While the rest of the Venerable Fly Tyers catch six-inch tiddlers on number twenty dry flies in full daylight, Doc Scott naps. He stores up reserves for the pursuit of twenty-inch brown trout after dark. Then while the Fly Tyers sip their whiskey and regale each other with stories of the big one—a seven-inch brookie—that got away, he eases out into a familiar stretch of water and plies its tenebrous edges with a big floating hairball of fly he calls a 'Night Stalker.'

"On one such outing, I was ceremoniously invited to accompany him, an honor few ever receive. We fished a familiar stretch of water just above Doc's cabin. It was a warm June night; a sulphur spinner fall had ended an hour earlier. Doc and I sat on a tussock of grass-covered bog in midstream waiting for coal darkness and the sound of a big brown rising to clean up the sulphurs that had drowned and clumped in back eddies.

"I produced my flask from the hidden pocket in my fishing vest and offered a toast. You know, my usual one: 'To the River Gods ... slurp ... and the fly-fishermen that have gone before us ... slurp ... and those that will come after ... slurp ... slurp.' Doc knows that fishing is always better after a toast and enthusiastically shared my bone medicine.

"Then, we eased off our roost and into the murky current of the Au Sable River. Doc worked down and began casting midstream to water behind another tussock, similar to the one we had just vacated. I moved up a bit and fished to back eddies under the alders. Soon Doc felt a tug on the end of his line and set the hook vigorously. Faster than a bobcat on a rabbit, the raucous honking of an angry goose split the night air. Doc had missed his mark in the darkness and landed his fly on the nesting bird. The fight of a lifetime ensued, as the panicked goose went this way and that, with more power than a forty-pound salmon—or a forty horsepower Mercury outboard for that matter. Try as he might, he couldn't separate his line from the goose. So, he pointed his rod at it, pulled it taut, and gave it a tug that he thought would surely break the tippet. But the tippet held!

"Pricked even deeper, the goose launched herself into the air. Line was screaming out now at an overhead angle. Never before had Doc been into his backing with the rod pointing straight up. Never before had he had a fight like this. Yet he played the flying goose masterfully and eventually settled it back on the water.

"At the first sound of that battle, I hustled down to Doc's position. Slowed by waist-deep water and uncertain footing in the darkness, I arrived at his shoulder just as the goose had stopped thrashing. We switched on our headlamps and peered into the gloaming. Forty feet ahead lay the goose on the water, wrapped in fly line and just barely able to keep her head up. We approached her cautiously, Doc reeling in slack as we went. Exhausted, the goose lay limp in a clump of entangled orange fly line. Doc carefully picked her up and cradled the still creature, as we began to unwrap line from the goose. We were nearly done—just one strand over her neck remained. As Doc removed the last thread, the goose suddenly came to life and raised her head. If you can imagine an angry goose, in the light of your headlamp, looking at you eyeball to eyeball, with a big, powerful beak just inches away, you have the picture.

"What happened next was a blur. Doc screamed, the goose screamed, wings spanned and beat, and the goose was away again. Although the fly line had been untangled, the hook was still deep in goose flesh!

"The fight was briefer this time around, before the goose settled twenty feet out on the water. She then took a long look at her tormentor with the small light on his head. Then, with wings flapping and legs kicking, she headed right for him. When she struck, her beak was at just the right height to hit a startled, back-stepping Doc in his most delicate anatomy. But one blow wasn't enough; she wasn't done. On the water right there, she hit him again and again with the axe-like swing of her long neck. Finally, her vengeance slaked, she was off, airborne and straightaway. The line tightened, and finally the tippet broke."

That was the end of the telling, and I don't know where the story goes from there. I imagine that Bald Eagle put his arm around his friend and helped him back to the tussock. There, he undoubtedly produced the flask from its hidden pocket. He held his buddy's shaking hands and raised the drink to his lips. They would sit for a long time in the calming darkness, before giving up the quest for big browns that night. If any promise of secrecy was sworn, it was soon forgotten, as this story has been told over and over again whenever the Venerable Fly Tyers met.

I suspect that it has also been told in the cattails and rice beds of goose circles. About the night the man called "little-light head" stung and lassoed Maud and pulled her around on a tether. How her brave and swift attack had inflicted pain of a special kind. How her heroic stand for all of goosedom got the better of the man and all mankind!

I know this story was told in those circles, because no one can "make crap" better than a goose!

# THE FISHMASTER

"It rides like a hooked fish in the current," said Bald Eagle, as we headed north on I-75. A bit of wind had come up, and I slowed down a little to control the swaying. "Are you sure the truck is big enough for this?" he asked.

"Sure it is. It's a half-tonner, and the camper can't weigh more than five hundred pounds," I said with more confidence than I felt. It was still early in my fly fishing development then and one of the first Fishwagon jaunts up north—kind of a shakedown trip for both the Fishwagon and me.

Finally, I found a smooth ride at about fifty-five miles per hour. Car after car passed us, the drivers with their necks craned to get a good look at the Fishwagon. "See how they look at us with pure envy," I said.

"If mouths open and brows furrowed is envy, you're right," Bald Eagle muttered.

Soon a guy in an SUV passed us, making wild gestures. "He wants us to pull over," said Bald Eagle. "Something must be wrong."

I followed the SUV onto the shoulder. I was quick to hop out and see what was the matter. We met between vehicles, before he led me to the rear of mine. "Say fella, you're sure putting out a lot of smoke from your exhaust there."

"All the time?" I asked.

"Now that you mention it, just when you are going uphill. Maybe you are giving it a little gas then, eh?"

Giving it a little gas? Hell, I was flooring it. Hmm … and that made it smoke! When I climbed back into the truck, Bald Eagle asked, "What's up?"

"Nothing, that guy just said it smokes a bit when we go uphill."

"A bit?"

"Well, a lot. You know, when I punch it."

So on we went. I tried to gain speed prior to each hill so I could go lighter on the gas. Soon, a guy pulled up alongside us in a brand new Hummer, looked at us and laughed, then passed and settled back into our lane, not more than two car lengths ahead.

"Pass him quick," said Bald Eagle. And I did.

"Now, Archer, punch it and smoke the bastard!"

We would smoke several bastards in the next two hours. It seemed that the road was full of them—what fun!

After our bastard-smoking marathon, we drove down Stephan Bridge Road and pulled into Gates Au Sable Lodge. It was a busy place during fishing season, and the only parking spot left was right next to the fly shop.

"Let's ask Rusty for a fishing report, but first we'll buy some flies," said Bald Eagle. Rusty Gates was still alive then and proprietor of his family's fishing lodge.

We tie our own flies, but never would we ask the owner of a fly shop for a fishing report without first purchasing something—and it sure wasn't going to be a new fly rod every time!

Rusty tied some of the finest flies anywhere. In those days of imports, Rusty and several of his employees and buddies spent the winter in the "Boardroom" above the garage next to the shop. They hole up in there like a bunch of monks transcribing Holy Writ. With heavy snow falling outside, a wood-burning stove in the corner, and a pot of chili slowly cooking on its top, they tied the hundreds of dozens of flies that would be sold during the fishing season in his fly shop.

Of course, he was more than happy to show us what was working and tell us the time of day to use them.

Only after the selection was made and money exchanged, did I ask, "Rusty, where should we go and use these flies? Where are the fish hitting?"

He looked at me, then out the window, then back at me. "Is that your vehicle out there, the one with the old beat-up camper on it—parked in front of my lodge?"

"Yup, it's my new Fishwagon. And, I ..."

"North Branch," he interrupted, "way up on the North Branch."

"Is that far away?" I asked.

"Yah, real far."

So off we went, new flies in hand, headed for a destination that was sure to work. After all, Rusty himself sent us there!

After about a thirty-minute drive, we turned off the pavement and onto a bumpy two-track. A few turns and ruts later, we pulled into a primitive camping area with just three sites, a shared outhouse, and a water pump. A tent was set up in one so we took the one next to it and closest to the stream.

"It's almost six o'clock; let's eat first and then go fishing," said Bald Eagle. "How are we going to cook?"

"We could use the gas stove inside or the charcoal grill out here," I answered.

"Let's cook out here. I'll start the charcoal; you get the food. By the way, what are we having?" asked Bald Eagle.

"Bratwurst, baked beans, and cream-style corn—washed down with copious amounts of the Angler's Ale you so graciously brought."

Later, after a few healthy draughts, I asked him, "Why do the Venerable Fly Tyers call you 'The Fishmaster?'"

"Whoever catches the most fish of the day is called 'The Fishmaster'—sometimes that's me," he said.

I would later find out from other members of the Venerable Fly Tyers that it wasn't sometimes him, it was always him. He simply knew how to find and catch fish better than anyone else. Most fly-fishermen go through a progression: catch a fish, catch lots of fish, catch a big fish, catch lots of big fish. But Bald Eagle's progression was off the chart. He had passed through all those stages long ago. Now, he just wanted to catch smart fish, educated fish, what he called "PhD fish." A fish, for example, who chooses a lie in a corner of logs with two branches over its head. It sits there comfortably in a slow, steady current that funnels big bugs right into its waiting maw. It has plenty of time to look at them and it won't be fooled easily. Casting is nearly impossible with any fast current between you and it. The fly must be put on a dime. And then, if you can even get the fly to the PhD fish, it better be a perfect imitation and not have the least bit of micro drag or you'll put the fish down. While the rest of us would lose several flies and at least two leaders on a fish like that, Bald Eagle routinely catches it. "The Fishmaster" indeed!

After dinner we donned our waders, rigged our fly rods, and trekked upstream from the campground. Bald Eagle selected a spot where the river widened and was less cluttered with brush. I was new to fly fishing then, and he knew this would help my casting. Bald Eagle found a few small fish rising to a bug he called "sulphurs." I tied on the number sixteen Roberts Yellow Drake that he handed me and began casting across the stream to several rising fish.

After he watched me hook a fish or two, Bald Eagle moved downstream and left me to it. I hooked a couple more before I noticed a fish rising above me. It was tight against the bank and in the same current seam that I stood in. At that time, I only knew how to cast to fish across the stream from me, so I tried to wade across to the other side. But the water proved too deep. So I returned to my original position and tried to cast to the fish above. I succeeded only in splashing the water over its head, and soon it stopped rising.

About then, Bald Eagle returned to check on me. I told him about my problem cast. He advised me to put on some extra tippet. "Cast to the side of the fish a bit," he said. "Stop the cast high and let the fly gently float down above and in-line with the fish." I tried a couple of times, but just wasn't getting it.

"Let me show you," he said. We traded places and he made a gentle upstream cast. His fly line touched down on the water lightly, about two feet to the right of the fish's last rise. The fly then fluttered to the surface like a wounded butterfly, three feet above and two feet to the left of the line. I watched it drift … three feet … two feet … one foot … then the fish rose and confidently took the fly. Fishmaster indeed!

"Archer, there is another riser in the same seam, twenty feet above," said Bald Eagle. "Why don't you move up a bit and give it a try?"

So I did. My second cast laid out perfectly, and after a brief fight, I held an eight-inch brook trout in my hand. I took a long look, admiring its beauty and glistening colors. As I released it, I thought, "I wonder if it sees me as a tormentor or a liberator. It probably can't make the connection that I tied the fake that brought it to my hand. But in the end, it must know that I released the hook from its lip and gently set it free."

Then, I watched it sit at my feet for a bit. Perhaps it was just catching its breath, or maybe … it liked me!

Bald Eagle parted and waded downstream around the bend. I found more rising fish and was able to cast to them no matter their position: above, below, or across. After an hour or so, the fish quit rising. I fished the water, the likely lies that Bald Eagle had taught me might hold trout but had no luck.

I wondered how my companion was doing, so I got out of the water on the near bank and quietly walked downstream. Around the second bend, I saw Bald Eagle. He was releasing a good fish, a twelve-incher, a brown trout I surmised from the glimmer of yellow that I saw. Not knowing that I was watching him, he nevertheless put on a clinic. Over the course of the next half hour, I observed him do all the things that he once told me a great fly-fisher did. "Great fly-fishers move through the water with the patience and stealth of a heron; they make no wake. Every footfall is carefully calculated to find the fish and position to cast. They crouch, stay low, and slide along the backdrop of streamside vegetation. By minimizing their presence, they gain total awareness of their surroundings. They become predators, pure and simple. They cast infrequently, but when they do, it is always to a fish and right on target. They have already planned the fight and quickly bring the fish into slack water away from any trouble or hang-ups. They gently net it and release it away from the water from which they took it."

Yes, we fly-fishers are predators, but the objective of our predation is not to kill and eat our prey, but to trick it into taking fake bugs, then to dance with it a while, bring it to hand, admire its beauty, and finally set it free. Hopefully, both learn a lesson—the fish to be more circumspect, the fisher-man to live in the fullness of the moment.

Later that summer, we returned to Gates Au Sable Lodge. The parking spot in front of the fly shop was open and I took it—it seemed to have my name on it. After purchasing a few flies, we approached Rusty to ask him where we should go fishing this time.

"You're back," he said, "I thought I sent you and that camper to the North Branch."

"That was three weeks ago," I said. "Where should we go this time?"

"Try the South Branch by Chase Bridge," he quickly answered.

"Is that far?" I asked.

"Yah, real far."

After driving to Chase Bridge, we drove up the Mason Tract Trail and found a campsite at Canoe Harbor.

"It's almost six o'clock; let's eat first and then go fishing," said Bald Eagle. "I'll start the charcoal, you get the food. By the way, what are we having?"

"Bratwurst, baked beans, and cream-style corn," I said.

"We had that last time," he said. "Why are we having it again?"

"Because I like bratwurst, and I'm not allowed to eat it at home," I said. "And here, there are no wives to tell us we can't. Did you bring that Angler's Ale again?"

A month later we were on our way north again. This time Bald Eagle drove, because my truck broke down at the last minute and was in the shop for repairs. With no camper, we decided to rent a room at Gates Au Sable Lodge.

After registering and buying a few flies, I asked Rusty, "Where should we fish—the North Branch? South Branch?"

He quickly looked over the parking lot and then answered, "Why don't you fish right out front of your room—best fishing on the river!"

# THE CARP AWARD

"Give it to Ken. Yes, let's give it to Ken!" chorused the Venerable Fly Tyers as they called for the official vote for the year's Carp Award.

Several years had passed since the Carp Award was first presented in jest at the Fly Tyers annual Christmas Party, when it was playfully substituted for the Sportsman's Award and a brook trout picture became a carp picture. After the ruse was exposed, all thought that it was a great idea to make it an annual presentation. The criterion was "*To the Man Who Did the Most to Ensure the Fish Got Away,*" in other words, to the biggest screwup of the year. Needless to say, we had more fun with this award than any of the others. The Big Fish Award, the Fly Tyer Award, and the Sportsman's Award were all earned, but the Carp Award was bestowed.

Since then, many of the Fly Tyers have proudly displayed the Carp Award in their home or office, on the mantel or on a prominent wall. Only one member hid it in shame in his closet all year. That intrepid angler won it for shouting at two fellow members of the Venerable Fly Tyers, who had the audacity to canoe around a blind corner and right through his salmon hole. He threw such a rod-breaking tantrum that he didn't even recognize his fellow club members. They could still hear him shouting and cursing as they drifted around the next several bends.

I even won the darn thing once. I was salmon fishing on the Clinton River with Dean Mettam when I got a hit while working a near-bank hole with a pair of deep-running nymphs. I set the hook and fought the "fish" for fifteen minutes. It never moved upstream or down but pulled back and forth, thumping like a good mouth-hooked fish. Mettam was so convinced that I had on a salmon that he climbed up onto the bank to net it for me. On his hands and knees, he crept into position, carefully positioned his net, and precariously leaned over to look down into the water. Startled, he looked again. Then he laughed heartily and reported that I was hooked to part of a tree that was flexing back and forth in the current. Mettam, of course, nominated me at that year's Christmas Party for a long and gallant fight with a root. And … I nominated him for trying to net said root. A long discussion followed, a vote was taken, and a deadlock declared. The resolution … the award would be shared by the offending parties.

Ken Miller, the champion of the Carp Award, has won it no fewer than five times. His first victory occurred during the club's annual trip west, to Yellowstone National Park. We had hiked six miles into the backcountry to fish our favorite water, a stream profuse with sixteen- to eighteen-inch, pure Yellowstone cutthroat trout. It is usually the best fishing of the trip. After the long hike in, we dropped our daypacks, pulled a long draught from our water bottles, and then suited up to fish. Ken let out a sorrowful moan and said, "Oh no, I left my waders back at the car."

Oh, he fished all right. The water was too cold to wet wade, so Ken crept along the high, grassy bank, trying to cast down to the stream four feet below. He hooked fish but landed none. Fish and flies were lost as he tried to raise them to his terrestrial perch on the 6x tippet required to hook them in the first place.

The next year, Ken won the award again. He earned the honor not fifty feet from where he won it the year before. In preparation for the trip, Ken, a company rep for 3M, had purchased two new Scientific Angler reels and fly lines from the employee store. Waders on this time, he clambered down the bank and into the stream. When he attempted his first cast, we heard him cry out, "I can't believe it—I wound my line on backwards."

"Try the other reel, Ken!" we shouted. He did and soon said, "Oh no, it's backwards, too." He had wound them both backwards and, for his punishment, spent the next hour under the shade of a cedar stripping out line and backing—then rewinding, along with bits of dirt, grass, and twigs, while the other Fly Tyers caught fish after fish from the big hole right in front of Ken.

Then there was the day the Venerable Fly Tyers were fishing the South Branch of the Au Sable River. We had planned a full day's wade requiring two cars. Ken had a brand new vehicle and was a bit persnickety about it. The shorter drive on the dusty gravel road was to the downstream takeout, so we left Ken's car there. He made a bit of a fuss about where to leave his key and ended up putting it in his pocket. A fine arrangement, assuming, of course, he didn't drown and we couldn't find his body. What we didn't know was that later, for reasons we still don't understand, he placed his key in the glove box of Mettam's car, which we left at the upstream end.

It was a gorgeous day, and the Fly Tyers were thick into fish. Ken, a fantastic fisherman, caught more than anyone. About three hours into the wade, Ken and I rested on a streamside log. I mentioned that I was glad we had his new car waiting for us at the end of the wade. "It will save a long walk back to Mettam's car," I said.

A panicked look blossomed on Ken's face, he abruptly rose, headed into the woods, and shouted back over his shoulder, "I'll catch up with you, don't worry!"

Two hours later he broke through the streamside brush and clomped into the river beside me. His face was hot and red and he had heavy sweat rings under the arms of his tech fishing shirt. I had been worried and wondered where he had been. He explained that he had gone after the key, and he was darn lucky that Mettam left his car unlocked.

A few minutes in the cool stream seemed to set him right, or so I thought. Eventually, he broke away from me and continued fishing downstream. Not fifteen minutes later, I rounded a bend and witnessed the strangest thing I have ever seen on a trout stream. Two wader-clad fishermen were jumping up and down in a foot of water, like popping corn in a frying pan. They were Ken and Mettam, and they were trying to reach a fly rod that was suspended high in an overhanging cedar. I sauntered over to my leaping companions, nonchalantly reeled in my line so that my fly was an inch or two out of the top guide, reached up, hooked the suspended rod, and pulled it down.

"Whose rod was it anyway?" I asked the sheepish pair and should have known the answer.

"Mine," said Ken, "I hooked my fly in the cedar on a backcast and couldn't pull it out. So I tightened the line, pointed my rod at the fly, and pulled hard to break the tippet. I guess my hand was wet, because I lost hold of the grip and the bent bough just sprung my fly rod up there!"

Ken got the only two nominations for the Carp Award that year. The Fly Tyers had some difficulty deciding which nomination would prevail. So, he won the award in a new category, as a *"Multiple Event Violator of Good Sense!"*

Another year went by, and at the Venerable Fly Tyers' Christmas Party, several members were nominated for the Carp Award but not Ken. No one had a story of another of his streamside screwups. Just when it looked like we might break his string and have to give the award to someone else, Ken's wife, Donna, spoke up … she wanted to nominate Ken for the award. This was an unprecedented turn of events. The rule said that the nomination had to come from a member. But, dying to hear what this was going to be, we had a quick vote and extended nominating privileges to wives.

Donna related an animated story of fishing the Colorado River with Ken. "We hired a guide and drifted the river for hours without so much as a hit. As we entered a fast-flowing section, Ken got a strike. He set the hook hard and it looked like a good fish. I worried about the current, but the guide expertly stopped the boat and held it in steady in the flow. Ken skillfully played the 'fish,' and soon brought it to the net. But, the 'fish' was not a cutthroat, not a rainbow, not even a rare greenback trout. It was a Coney Island whitefish," she said, and burst into laughter.

Now, you adults know what she was talking about … and you youngsters, it's just as well you don't. Suffice it to say, Ken won the Carp Award again.

The fifth time Ken won the award was because of something that occurred on another Yellowstone trip. All week, we kept watch on Ken to see what he would do. Expectations were high. Everyone wanted to fish with him. We watched in eager, almost giggling, anticipation. But Ken let us down. He had his waders, his fly line was wound correctly, he entered the stream and moved about the water cautiously. When he snagged a fly in a tree, he held onto the rod carefully. In short, he could do no wrong. The week went by and the only thing that we witnessed was Ken catching one heck of a lot of fish!

At the end of the week, we left the park and made the scenic drive back to Billings over Beartooth Pass. We recalled the screwups of other club members, thinking Ken was out of the woods and that we would have to give the award to someone else. At the top of the pass, we pulled over for a pit stop. Captivated by the view, we stood there and took our relief. The wind was strong and we had all turned our backs to it. That is all … but Ken. Facing the full gale, his stream arced out and back onto his foot. Mike Hrabonz (RAY-bonz) noticed it first. Giggling and pointing, he directed our gaze to Ken, just as Ken felt the wet in his sock. It is hard to describe his reaction—like the dance of a disjointed contortionist at a Grateful Dead concert. In one Gordian move, he had to stop the flow, get out of the wind, move his leg out of the way, and protect what he held in his hand! That dance, accompanied by a surprised, moaning croak, had the rest of us on the ground rolling in laughter. Technically, Ken hadn't done anything to "insure the fish got away," but that was just too good not to earn the award.

That December, at the annual Christmas Party of the Venerable Fly Tyers, a motion was made and unanimously passed to rename the Carp Award to the "Ken Miller Award!"

# DAN WAS RIGHT

In the duck marshes of Michigan, we anxiously await the rising of the sun. This is when shooting begins and all the preparation of the past few hours meets the expectation of the morning hunt. Up to now, darkness has reigned. In darkness, we counted our shells, loaded the boat, and found our way through two miles of cattail channels and cuts. Then we spread our decoys with care, and set our stations with the two-by-four tees that we use as stools and the plastic bread trays for footing in the seemingly bottomless mud.

And, then we wait!

On a cloudy day, the kind that you hope to have in the duck marsh, you can't tell exactly when sunrise occurs. At first, a heavy blanket of darkness confines you. You can see only a foot or two ... your hands, slightly lighter than the dark walnut of your shotgun, and the cocoon of cattails immediately surrounding you. Slowly, with the day's increasing light, your world starts to expand. More things appear. The cattail sentinels become an army of narrow stalks with fat heads swaying in the early breeze. The nearest decoy comes into view. Slowly you begin to count them, one by one, out the chain until you see the last vanguard of your spread. You think you see a dark object streak by overhead, but you're not sure. Then another. Ducks perhaps, but too soon to shoot. You hope they will come back; you hope that they aren't the only ones you will see, for you know that opening hour is the best time of the day for a duck hunt.

Slowly the entire marsh comes to life. Red-winged blackbirds that have been roosting in nearby cattails begin to stir and chirp. What kind of memory does a bird have? Does it remember yesterday's sunrise? Or perhaps the sun wakes it, and it is like waking for the first time. It chirps, "What is this? I'm warm now and I can see. Isn't this grand? Let's fly around, meet our neighbors, and celebrate!"

The shift from darkness to light, from cold to warm, must be a monumental event for all creatures living in the wild—not just the promise of another day, but a rebirth. *CREATION* didn't occur just once in seven days, it occurs each and every day in the duck marsh with the rising of the sun!

I hunt to be part of the pageant of dawn. Where else can you spend an entire hour experiencing the sunrise, without even seeing the sun?

When it was light enough to see the cattails beyond the break of our spread, Ducker whispered, "Do you have your watch? Is it time to shoot yet?"

"Another five minutes," I said. The words were hardly out of my mouth when we heard shots from across the marsh.

"I say it's officially shooting time," said Ducker. "That other guy must have a better watch than that cheap, pilot one of yours—big on the wrist, small on accuracy."

Then Ducker said, "Get ready, here they come," and raised his gun. I saw a brace of mallards appear out of the gloam from his side. It was too early to tell whether they were drakes or hens, but since they were our first, it didn't matter. Ducker dropped the first bird and I took the trailer on my second shot. No sky-busting here; the low light forces you to take them in close, and they don't fall far! We gathered them quickly, a drake and a hen. A quick high five and we were back at our posts, waiting for the next incomers.

Ducker is my boon hunting companion. He introduced me to the St. Clair Flats, that magic stretch of duck marsh north of Detroit and along the waterway between Michigan and Ontario. On the other side of the St. Clair River, just two miles away as the duck flies, is Walpole Island. There, rich guys hunt with native guides over baited fields. They enjoy the more generous Canadian limits and take many ducks.

But we are content on our side, for it is the camaraderie and the calling of our own ducks that count most for us. To make our own hunt, that is our way.

Ducker taught me most of what I know about duck hunting. He is an optometrist by profession, a duck hunter by choice ... quick to trade a white smock for long johns and a camo jacket.

And so went the morning, a flurry of ducks and shooting for the first hour, tapering off as the sun climbed and lit the marsh. As the sun burned through the overcast, the ducks climbed higher and were able to better detect the groupings of dark blocks scattered through the marsh as the fakes that they were.

A lull set in. We removed a layer of clothing as the morning warmed. I poured a cup of coffee from my thermos, munched on a candy bar refugee from Halloween, and settled back.

I knew what was coming. Ducker began to get "twitchy." He looked at our spread and suggested ways to improve it. I argued that it brought ducks in earlier and there were none overhead now. But I knew that I was only postponing the inevitable—he did this on every hunt.

Then, a duck came in ... low, alone, and unseen until it dropped to the water seventy yards left of our decoys. "That settles it," Ducker whispered. "We've got to move them; they're in the wrong place." So out we trundled, through the calf-deep muck of the marsh. We grabbed several decoys each by their cords and moved them the seventy yards to where the lone duck had come in, flushing it as we went. It took three trips and another one to gather our tees, shotguns, and bread trays. Ducker made one more trip out to adjust the deeks a bit. Set up over the new spread, we were now overheated and tired. Yet, Ducker had a satisfied look on his ruddy face. But, it didn't last long, vanishing as soon as another lone duck came in and landed—you guessed it—right where the decoys had been!

Two hours later we were still sitting ... and still waiting for more ducks to show up. We saw a few passersby in the distance. Some just toured the marsh before returning to the refuge. Some dropped into other hunters' spreads and were never seen again. But none came our way. Perhaps we should have packed it in, but we were reluctant to leave. "We might miss something," Ducker always said.

Then, behind us and far out I see a duck. With the wind at our back and decoys in front, this upwind bird is not likely to come in. But I continue to watch it, sneaking peeks from our vigil over the decoys, not wanting Ducker to know.

Ducker is busy trying to light a cigarette. He isn't good at it. Not in the wind anyway, because he doesn't smoke. Doesn't smoke except in the duck blind. It is the same with me—a bowl of pipe tobacco, outdoors only, not often, not habitual, not addicted. The way Native Americans originally used tobacco, something savored and enjoyed on special occasions.

The duck is closer now … maybe coming our way. I think of calling, but then Ducker would know. As usual, he is ahead of me in the duck count. A better shot, a better hunter! But what I lack in shooting skills, I make up for by usually seeing the ducks first. My pilot-trained eyes are conditioned to looking for specks on the horizon and, just as importantly, looking away for others and coming back. We call that track-while-scan. It is what fighter aircraft radar does. Not many hunters do that. They fix on one set of birds, unaware of the lone one sneaking in from the side, or in this case, the rear. Another peek … this bird is definitely coming in. It's close enough now to make out … a hen mallard, lonely and looking for solace in a spread of fakes.

I should warn Ducker, but I don't. This is my chance and I'm going to make the most of it. I will wait until the hen is well within range, and then I will turn, take careful aim, and drop her. Ducker will be caught with his half-lit cigarette hanging from his chapped lips. And, he will be awed by his companion's apparent quick sighting and deadeye. Perhaps he will be kind enough to retrieve the bird. I will not tell him of how I waited, how I connived, and how low my motives were!

Ducker starts to stir. He has given up on the cigarette and is beginning to look around. I can wait no longer. I turn and shoot, an easy shot, but I hurry it and miss.

It is hard to know what happened next. Thinking back on it, I know that the first shot was mine alone, and the second shot was a simultaneous blast from both our cannons. The duck folded, fell, and crashed hard to the water; she was hit by the heart of the load.

But, whose load? Ducker and I looked at each other, and both wanted to ask, "Who shot that bird? Was it you or me?" But after years of hunting together, we no longer ask that question. It's impossible to answer. Better for each to think privately that he hit the duck and the other guy missed it. Or be generous and think that we both hit the bird. In this case, we probably did, the way she went down.

Instead, another question emerged from Ducker's lips. "She was going left-to-right, wasn't she?"

"She was going straight up when you first saw her," I said. "Before that she was going right-to-left."

"I'm sure she was going left-to-right," Ducker argued.

"Listen, Ducker. I'd been watching her a long time, and she was going right-to-left!"

"You had been watching her ... a long time?" he said accusingly. "Then you would think you would have been more accurate in determining the direction of her flight and might have hit her with the first shot!"

I had been busted, my low character exposed. He was right about the first shot but not the direction of flight. But he held the moral high ground, and I knew when to retreat. He stood in a self-righteous silence while I went off to retrieve the bird.

When I brought it back to our spot in the cattails, he took part in examining the prize.

"She is a fine bird," Ducker said. "You can tell from her weight and those orange legs, she's a flight bird. Probably lost her mate and was looking for company. Good thing you saw her early, or she could have blown right through without either of us getting a shot."

It's hard to stay mad at a guy like that. He had already forgiven me for trying to keep the bird to myself. Oh hell, he probably did kill it. I missed the first shot and most likely the second as well. I'm sure he killed it!

When it came time to pick up the decoys, I hustled to do more than my share. I wound the cords, bagged them, and tossed them into the boat. He retrieved our wooden seats and pried the bread racks from the mud. As usual he drove the boat—my boat, his motor, partnered up like us. He graciously divided the ducks equally, and we each set out for our homes in good cheer.

Normally, that would be the end of the story. But what happened at each of our homes must be reported! When Ducker regaled his wife with the tale of our hunt and the part about which way the duck was flying, she responded, "Now Dan, you know Dave is a pilot; he sees things better than you do. I'm sure Dave was right!"

How quickly our wives think we are wrong and the other right. Perhaps they know us too well, for in my house it went like this: "Now Dave, you know Dan is an eye doctor; he sees things better than you do. I'm sure Dan was right!"

# WIVES, CHILDREN, AND FISHING

My wife says that it is a shame that I haven't devoted the same effort to my family and church as I have to fly fishing. That simply is not true, dear! Have you forgotten the time I took the family to the Circus Museum in Baraboo? Or all those dance recitals I attended? Why, I even put down my fly fishing magazine while our girls were on stage! And I tried to teach the girls fishing, but they were already ruined by the instant gratification they got in all those trips to the mall with you. They never could understand catch and release. As you have said yourself, "How could they apply that concept to shopping or finding a husband?"

I'm offended by your comment that the biggest smile you have ever seen on me was in that picture where I held a turkey in one hand and a steelhead in the other. While that was a great day, I have smiled equally big on many occasions with you. Although, I admit, it might have been too dark for you to see.

And as for church, fishing is a spiritual experience. It is no accident that Jesus chose his apostles from among fishermen or that some of his miracles involved multiplying fish. With more faith, Peter could have walked on water and saved himself the trouble of using a boat.

Of course, honey, I love you more than fishing, and just as soon as I get back from this trip, I'm going to tell you about it!

# THE RILEY NEWMAN LETTERS

The Venerable Fly Tyers pulled into Cooke City, Montana, on our annual Yellowstone fishing trip. We passed the police car parked on the east edge of town and reduced speed. We knew that it was a fake but slowed anyway out of respect for the town's ingenuity. This small mountain village of a hundred and fifty souls, just outside the Northeast Gate to Yellowstone National Park, could not afford a police force. So, they cleverly bought, on the cheap, a couple of old cruisers and parked one at each end of the single street that went through town. Inside was a dark plywood silhouette of a cop, complete with his broad-brimmed hat, one hand on the steering wheel, the other holding a donut—okay, I'm making up the donut part. Nevertheless, a sidelong glance at the vehicle was convincing enough and helped keep down the speed of passing cars and the many motorcycles that passed through here each summer on their annual pilgrimage to Sturgis.

After checking into our cabins at the Antlers Lodge, we walked two blocks to dine at the Bistro. "Dine" may be too fancy a word for Cooke City; "chow down" would be more appropriate. Over the years, we found that we couldn't count on consistently good food from any of the half dozen restaurants in town. One year, one would stand out and the next year another …

or none. We chalked it up to the difficulty of attracting and retaining cooks for such a short season.

Wait staff was also hard to obtain and usually brought in from the outside. Often they were from Europe, sponsored by some international work program that brought young people to work summer jobs, see the country, and hopefully go back with a favorable impression of America. This year the girls working at the Bistro were from the Czech Republic.

"Tell me, Milena, what was America like?"

"It's a funny place, Vojtech, all mountains and old, wooden buildings. Some of the people wear leather clothes and ride something called a 'Harley.' Others, the strangest of all, wear rubber pants, and sleeveless jackets with many pockets full of weird things. They carry long whips and smell like fish!"

The Bistro was owned and operated by a man we called "Frenchy" because of his accent and Continental élan. His wife worked the cash register and was naturally "Mrs. Frenchy." After lunch, as we paid our bill, Hrabonz asked her if there was any place in town where we could buy some trout flies.

"Yes," she replied. "Riley, the guy who runs the laundromat, sells them. Follow me!" And, with that, we were out the door and walking down the street. We climbed the uneven steps to an old, western, false-fronted building and found the door to the laundromat closed and locked. Mrs. Frenchy then led us around the building to the back where she picked up pebbles and tossed them at an upstairs window. I don't even want to surmise how she knew to do that or at which window to toss them. But soon a sleepy-eyed face appeared behind the glass. She shouted at the apparition, "Come down and open the store … you have customers!"

A few minutes later, a slim, somewhat disheveled fellow in an old sweatshirt and porkpie hat unlocked the front door and let us in. His name was Riley Newman. He was about thirty years old, unshaven, bleary-eyed, and obviously had just been sleeping off a bender. He led us through the entryway where a single coin-operated washer and dryer comprised the town's only laundromat. In the next room was a photo studio. Mounted on the walls were some of the finest outdoor photographs that I have ever seen,

large-formatted and rustically, yet artfully, framed. Riley Newman must
have trekked miles and sat for many hours to get the shots of bison, wolves,
and bear that adorned his studio walls.

In the corner of the studio was a small display case of flies. Riley moved
behind it. Puffed with obvious pride, he eagerly pointed out what he thought
might work at this time of year. He proudly proclaimed that he had tied all
the flies himself and based them on patterns he had seen at the fancy shops
in West Yellowstone. There were hundreds of flies in the case and they were
magnificent.

We each picked out a dozen or so, paid, and thanked him for the special
opening of his shop. We took our leave, but not before Hrabonz asked Riley
if he knew any good places to fish. He knew many but especially recommended the Yellowstone River below the Lamar confluence. "There are big
fish there," he said. "And not many people are willing to hike that far and
wade through the Lamar to get to it."

While driving into the park to fish a favorite stream, we marveled at
Riley Newman's three-in-one shop. He was obviously a troubled young
man, but his hand-tied flies and his art were first rate. We wondered what
demons drove him to try to eke out a living in such a backwater of the western landscape. Maybe we were just too citified to understand.

A couple of days later, looking for new water to fish, Hrabonz suggested we
give Riley's recommendation a shot. So off we headed. We pulled into the
off-road pullout just east of Tower Bridge. As we donned our waders for
the hike in, an old, rusty Buick, in a swirl of dust and hurry, slid to a stop
right next to us. Out jumped Riley Newman along with two other men.
Although we had just seen Riley two days prior, he maintained a formality
with us and even looked a bit chagrined that we were there. Maybe, when he
recommended the spot, he should have said, "Don't go there on Thursday.
I'm bringing guests!" Riley urged his crew to quickly don their gear and then
hustled them down the trail well ahead of us.

Shortly, we followed them, but they were soon out of sight. When we
came upon the Lamar, we got a glimpse of Riley and his buddies as they disappeared over the ridge on the other side. Two of the Venerable Fly Tyers,

Ken and Ron, elected not to cross but stay and fish the inviting boulder-strewn pools and pockets that abounded there. Meanwhile, Hrabonz and I tucked our vests inside our waders and, with elbows held high, inched our way through the chest deep water. On the far side, we climbed the ridge to the plateau above. We followed the Lamar to its junction with the Yellowstone and then down it. After about a quarter mile, from the vantage of a fifty-foot bluff, we saw Riley rigging up to fish the big water. Hrabonz mused, "I wonder which one of his beautiful flies he'll use today?"

"Look closely," I said. "It is not one that he showed us ... not one from his display case ... it's not even a fly. It's a long piece of wood with a lip and three treble hooks ... it's a Rapala!"

As we left the park a few days later, on the drive that took us over Beartooth Pass and back to Billings, we talked of many things. But Hrabonz kept coming back to Riley Newman, his shop, his flies, and that Rapala. Sometimes, a person can just get inside your head and you can't shake him loose. Perhaps you are just trying to understand what seems so foreign or incongruent about them. Or maybe wonder what it would be like to live like they do—maybe a bit of you would even like to give it a try. Hrabonz said that there was real talent wasted with Riley. That he knew people in his business of robotic design who made a fortune with only one-tenth the talent of a Riley Newman. That Riley could make a good living in that business or in fly fishing, for that matter, if he just had more ambition or had gotten the right start. He could be an innovative tyer, photographer, or guest speaker. "We could really use him at the Southfield Fly Fishing Show in March," Hrabonz concluded.

A week later, I was back to work, flying a five-day trip out of Detroit Metro. One leg took me through Minneapolis. I had a little extra time, so I went to the Billings gate and waited for the outbound crew. A few minutes later, I handed the captain a letter and asked him to post it for me from Billings,

so that it would display that city's postmark. It was addressed to Mike Hrabonz, and it said:

---

NEWMAN ENTERPRISES
131 FRONT ST
COOKE CITY, MT 59020

Dear Mr. Hrabonz,

My name is Riley Newman. I met your friends, Mr. Miller and Mr. Jankowski, on the Yellowstone River last September and they said you were "the
man" for fishing in Michigan. And if anyone could launch my career in fly
fishing, you would be the guy. They also said I met you in my shop in Cooke
City, but for some reason I don't remember it. Perhaps you do. I believe the
occasion was a special opening for your party at the request of the lovely wife
of the proprietor of the finest French restaurant in town. Remember me? I
was the fellow in the new sweatshirt and dapper hat.

Unfortunately, I was unable to hide my "Special Fly" from the keen-
eyed Mr. Jankowski. I am afraid now, that if the word gets out, it will spread
faster than gonorrhea in a whorehouse. If I am to get the credit that I deserve
for it, and since I am already somewhat of a celebrity in Cooke City, this
may be a propitious time to begin my career as a Fly Fishing Guest Speaker.
I understand you have quite a show in a field, south of Detroit, and that you
are in charge of it. Some of the ideas I have for my lectures are:

Rappin' with Riley
Flies of Finland
Three hooks are better than one
Yellowstone streamer fishing—how to get the wiggle
Big Flies plus Big Hooks equal Big Fish
Never use floatant again
Nymphing—Shmymphing
A simple fly box

However, since I am an ambitious man, that isn't all that I want to do. I
certainly don't want to give up my lucrative business here in Cooke City.

You know, the Studio, Fly Shop, and Laundromat! Your friends told me that you could help me in these areas as well. They said you are the "Robot Dude" for all Michigan. Some of the things that I was thinking I could use robots for are:

The Laundromat: I would like to buy another washer and double my production but am afraid the workload would be too much for me. Can robots load/unload washers and dryers? Can they put quarters in? How about soap? Can they sniff panties to be sure they are done?

The Fly Shop: Hogging out balsa wood is a tedious and tiresome task. A robot sure could help there. Do they come with magnetic fingers for picking up large hooks? Of course, I would expect to have to do myself the delicate tasks like spray painting, pasting on the eyes, and welding hooks by hand.
The Outdoor Photography Studio: Hiking up mountains at the crack of dawn to catch a beautiful sunrise over a pristine mountain valley, sunlight dappling tall trees, mist rising from the long grass, and a bear in the foreground caught in the delicate act of taking a crap sounds romantic but is hard work. Perhaps a well-designed robot could carry my gear. Can they be made to look like mules or alpacas—I don't want to be seen with a metal stick man walking beside me! Your robots are made of metal aren't they? I don't want the plywood kind the police department bought.

Domestic chores: It gets lonely in Montana in the winter. Perhaps you have a line of French robots, with long blonde hair and curves—hell, I'll take one that looks like a fat, old crone as long as it has a soft mouth!

Sincerely,
Riley Newman, Esq.
The Master of Balsa

And then, I waited. Tittering with anticipation, I pictured Hrabonz walking out to his mailbox, opening its little trap door, reaching in, and extracting his mail. As he walked back to the house, he would riffle through his letters and stop in his tracks when he saw the Newman Enterprises return address and the Billings postmark. He would eagerly rip open the envelope and read its contents. Hrabonz is smart and won't be fooled for long. But I would have loved to have been there to see his furled brow and pursed lips relax and open into a big, wide grin. "Gotcha!" I thought.

I hung by the telephone like a teenaged girl before prom, thinking he would call—disappointed when he didn't. Surely he would know it was from me! I squirmed like a worm on a hook, until finally, to my own mailbox came this answer:

---

Mr. Riley Balsa Newman
C/O Archer of the North
6072 Hickory Lane
Washington, MI 49094

Dear Mr. Newman,

Thank you so much for the flattering letter. I am honored to be selected the person to launch your career in fly fishing. I'm sorry you do not remember me, but I was the tall person in our group that was not scratching my private parts. I do remember your hat and purchased an exact replica upon my return to Detroit.

I am even more pleased that you have decided to enter the lecture circuit. I will act as your agent for a mere 5% of the balsa and laundry profits. I really enjoyed your suggested topics. Perhaps additional subjects you could cover are:

Balsa—Size does matter!!
Cardinal Newman—Paul Newman—Riley Newman (The Saint—The Actor—The Artist)
A woody a day keeps the flies away!

The robotic industry has long awaited your endorsement. In the past, we have assembled such mundane items as cars, home appliances, and aerospace components. We have yet to conquer the challenge of a Laundromat. I could see it now. A customer will walk into your fine establishment, a robot will roll him a cigarette, then as you suggested, we will design a special robot system to insert quarters into the washer and dryer. The robot will sort the clothes by color, or in your case smell, and add appropriate detergent (yes, you will have to use soap) and fabric softener (for the Montana gay community).

We have not designed an outdoor robot for your photography adventures, but our staff has a "domestic significant other" robot in development with you in mind. The Newman-matic will clean your studio, tie your flies, and wash your hat, and "take care" of your every need. All you have to do to turn her on is flip a switch. Of course, if it does not work out, she will take half of everything you own.

I look forward to meeting you again this year. I hope we will have a special opening as we did last year. I'm sure Mrs. Frenchy will make the arrangements.

Please let me know if you agree with my business proposal. We look forward to promoting the future of Newman Enterprises. Today Cooke City—tomorrow the world.

Sincerely,
Michael Hrabonz
Agent, Newman Enterprises

The next year, the Venerable Fly Tyers returned to Cooke City. The first thing we did was eagerly dash to Riley Newman's laundromat. Our excitement quickly faded when we saw that it was boarded up. We peeked through a slat and saw an empty building ... no washer and dryer, no wildlife photos, no display case of fine flies! Gone—all gone!

In dismay, we slowly made our way to the Bistro. Mrs. Frenchy didn't remember us. But when asked about Riley, she recalled with a faraway look and a tear in her eye, that he had been arrested late last year. It happened in Gardiner. He was drunk and got in a barroom fight. The fight moved outdoors, where Riley eventually ran over his antagonist with his car, backed it up, and did it again. Remarkably, the other guy lived, but Riley went to prison, now serving a six- to eight-year sentence for attempted murder.

Yes, over the winter, we had fun with our brief encounter with Riley ... exchanging letters and joking. One could even say that it was at his expense.

Yet, I wonder if it would have made a difference to him to know the high esteem we hold for his talents and the regard we have for him. We all touch so many lives, and Riley, unknown to him, had touched ours!

# ZEN AND THE ART OF FLY FISHING

R obert Pirsig published his book *Zen and the Art of Motorcycle Maintenance* in 1974. It was on the best-sellers list for decades, sold five million copies, and became a cult classic. Pirsig presented his philosophical ideas against the background of a seventeen-day motorcycle trip made with his son. I was young when I read it and confess to having missed many of the book's concepts, but I did take away the idea, as the book's title suggests, that even the mundane task of maintaining a motorcycle can be a zen-like experience.

"Zen" comes from the Japanese word *zazen* which in Buddhism simply means the practice of seated meditation. Traditionally it emphasizes various kinds of meditative techniques that essentially involve observing the mind. One technique that is commonly associated with zen is the use of the koan (KOH-on). A koan is a riddle that cannot be solved by the rational mind, so it forces the mind into a type of non-dual thinking to seek an answer.

Our Western minds think of zen without giving it a strict definition; instead, we get the feeling of being lost in form and nature. Without over-thinking it, we see something in its simplest terms and lose ourselves in that activity—what better than fly fishing?

Surrendering our problem-solving minds to the simple immersion experience of a beautiful stream, the motion of casting, and anticipation of a rising fish is a spiritual practice. We become lost in time and think, "Ah, this is zen!"

And if you want to practice a koan, here are two for you: Does a Woolly Bugger have a Buddha's spirit? What is the sound of one spinner falling?

# ODE TO THE LLAMA

Little Llama, why have you hidden so long in my fly box? Have you become lost under the ragged tails of longer streamers? Twenty years ago, I tied you: wisp of grizzly feather tail, gold tinsel over red floss, wing of woodchuck hair, and grizzly hackle collar. I put you in an obscure fly box corner where you have idly remained. Today, after not a single tug on my line and my fly patch filled with standards drying, I became desperate and pulled you out for the first time. You deftly plied the waters—ten fish in less than an hour! Were you telling me that I should have used you all along, that you deserved your own fly box row? You shall have it!

# CALL ME DEADEYE

I hate a braggart. I hate the way they boast about their big fish and how many points their buck had. It is even worse when they brag about how skilled they are with a rod or gun.

Now that I've said that, in this story, I do some bragging. But before you judge, let me say this: I am not a good shot! I have missed many ducks, partridge, and deer. In fact, I've missed many more than I have hit. But, then, "every dog has his day," and this was mine.

"You must be excited—it's your rookie deer hunt," said Ducker, as we pulled up short of the wire-and-pole gate after a four-hour drive.

"No, it's not. I've been up here hunting with you many times before," I said.

"That was bow hunting. This is your first rifle deer hunt. This is big time, 'Rookie.' Now get out and unlock the gate. Remember, swing it wide!"

I obliged. After all, I was his guest and he does so much to make this happen. Besides, I was anxious for a look at the property, or "Le Properte" as the Flick brothers call it. By any name, it is sixty acres of prime deer land near Evart in the heart of Michigan. Dan, aka Ducker, and his brother Bill picked it up for a couple hundred dollars an acre a few years back. It is worth more than five times that now. It amazes me how much is packed into this sixty-acre parcel. Beyond the gate stand the remains of an old homestead. An empty square of mature cottonwoods shade the remnants of the old stone foundation. Abandoned lilacs form a sentry line around its perimeter. The meadow beyond drops to a small pond that the brothers had dredged, then rises on the far side into a white pine stand. Beyond is a twelve-by-sixteen-foot cabin that the Flicks erected off the ground, deck-like. Made of two-by-fours and plywood, its rustic utility serves to keep the members of the hunt warm and dry. Completing the property is an old apple orchard, as well as stands of oak, beech, cedar, and hemlock in several low-lying, watery swales. The land undulates; walk fifty feet and it's different; walk another fifty feet and you cross two deer trails, one heavily used. This is a perfect place for game and much has been taken here.

Bill, who is always the first to arrive, greeted us at the cabin door. "I see you brought the rookie."

"I am not a rookie; I have been deer hunting many times with you before," I said.

"That was different; this is rifle hunting," he said as he began to help us with our load. Into the cabin went rifles, ammunition, sleeping bags, hunting clothes packed in separate bags complete with a variety of ways to hide odor, and enough food to feed twice our number for a month.

"The top bunk is yours again, Rookie," said Ducker.

"But the smoke from the stove collects up there," I protested.

"Yah, but so does the heat and that is why we give it to you, so you'll be warm and comfortable. We always give our guests the best bed in the house."

I hoisted my things onto the "best bed in the house," knowing there would be a night of coughing and choking ahead of me.

When things were unpacked, Ducker opened the cooler and passed Bill and me each a bottle of beer. He raised his bottle and said, "A toast to the rookie's first hunt."

I sipped the beer, unable to fight this any longer. Then we exchanged details of the drive up and our expectations for the morning. When the beer was gone, we busied ourselves around the cabin. Bill began preparing dinner, choice venison chops, taken earlier during bow season, along with potatoes and corn. He is an excellent outdoor cook. Dan and I hauled in firewood and kindling for the deadly pot-bellied stove in the corner, that belcher of smoke and fumes. "Creosote" is its middle name.

After dinner and more beer, we talked of the morning hunt. "Where are you set up, Bill?" asked Ducker.

"Down near the south fence, where I bow hunted," he answered. "I moved my rifle blind there last time I was up. How 'bout you?"

"I thought I'd shoot from the old blind that the porcupines chewed up, the one on the hill behind my bow blind. It's a little close to you though."

"That'll be all right, should be plenty of room and what one of us misses the other might get. Where should we put the rookie?"

"I was thinking the white pines blind, pretty open there, he should see deer once they start moving across the road from the field. Good shooting lanes, too … and none towards us," said Ducker.

That settled, Bill stoked the fire one more time and we prepared for bed.

As Bill eased into his sleeping bag on the low cot, he said, "I can't wait 'til tomorrow. November fifteenth is the biggest day of the year for me, bigger than Thanksgiving, bigger even than Christmas."

"Get a life," I thought. "It's just deer hunting." And then I remembered his history. Bill had been drafted during the Vietnam War and served in-country in the infantry. No telling what he saw—he never spoke of it. When he returned home a year later, he discovered that his young wife had left him. He never remarried or had children and has lived alone ever since. Feeling kindlier towards him, I silently hoped he would have a big opening day. Then I climbed up into my bed, took a deep breath and, holding it, fell asleep.

The five a.m. alarm mercifully awakened me from a bad dream. One in which I had been desperately trying to run away from a forest fire. With flames licking at my legs, they just wouldn't move.

Ducker's deft hand knocked the clock to the floor. Its vibrations picked up by bare plywood, the whole cabin rang. Bill, the first to pop up, was so eager and ready to go I think he must have slept in his hunting clothes. Ducker was next; he turned off the alarm and pulled on coveralls. Both brothers were out the door by the time I had hit the floor from my lofty perch.

The cool, fresh morning air never felt so good. With my rifle draped over my shoulder, I followed the entry road down to the white pines. Where the road turned left, I bore to the right, easing into the woods. The walking was easy here, as the mature pines shaded the forest floor, killing any undergrowth. A bright moon lit the way to the dark shape of the blind ahead.

Inside I sat on an old wooden chair and cradled the rifle in my lap. The gun felt good in my hands. It was still warm from a night in the cabin. It had belonged to the brothers' father, who after a long and brave struggle had recently succumbed to Parkinson's. The old thirty-thirty had seen a lot of hunts, and I had heard many stories of "Dad" shooting deer with it. Apparently he was as bad a shot as I am, once shooting the foot off a buck and then tracking it a long way before one of his boys finished it. I had no deer rifle of my own—thought I'd give this sport a try before laying down hard cash. I guess I was a rookie after all.

I fumbled through my right cargo pocket and extracted three cartridges—that should be enough. Loading the chamber, I felt privileged to use this gun. Although the brothers preferred their larger bore thirty-ought-sixes, this was a prized family heirloom. I had handled it once before, two weeks ago when Ducker and I took it to the range and sited it in. It had been dead on! Now I hefted it, brought it to my shoulder, cheek against the stock, and peered through the scope into the darkness. It felt good.

Soon my visual world grew as predawn light filtered through the white pines. Then came the magic hour … er, should I say minute. At precisely seven-oh-six a.m., the official opening time, I heard the first shot. It came from the west, maybe a half mile away, and was soon followed by many more. I don't know how far the sound of a shot will carry—a mile, maybe two. Of course, it depends on the wind, but what you gain in one direction, you lose in the other. By ten a.m., I had counted over eighty shots—eighty shots in a mile or two radius. There must be a lot of deer hunters out there and a lot of lead in the air.

I was wishing for a flak vest or a foxhole when my walkie-talkie crackled with the voice of Ducker saying, "Rookie, see any deer yet?"

"Nope, just heard a lot of shots," I answered. "Heard some from your direction, too. Get any?"

"Two down, we'll start tracking at noon. Say, why don't you move to my rifle blind on the east side of the property? Deer pile through there later in the morning; you might still see one."

Well, this spot had been a bust, so I got up and retreated through the white pines. As I passed the cabin, I began wondering, "Exactly where was that rifle blind he talked about?" Over the years, the Flicks had put up so many blinds, I wasn't sure.

Down the ridge between two wood duck swales, I jumped a rivulet and climbed a hill. Near the top sat an old, black-painted plywood blind. "This must be it," I thought, and settled in. The woods opened before me, one-hundred-and-fifty yards in all directions … except one. Fifty feet below and to the right, from the way I had come in, stood brush and low-lying shrubs.

Sunlight caressed the leafless trees as it passed through to the forest floor. I had been cold earlier, but the walk had warmed me. Three blue jays flew from the brushy spot and landed in a nearby popple. Always vocal, they squawked one of their many songs—easier to identify them by their strident voice than the tune. A red squirrel scampered down an oak and scolded the jays, then hopped about frantically looking for nuts. I smiled and thought, "This hyperactive child of the woods, if he were in grade school, he'd be on Ritalin."

The forest belongs to the one who has been there the longest and sits the quietest! Walk through and you might, if lucky, see movement far ahead … sit a half hour and it comes to life. I eased the rifle into the corner of the blind, sat back, and took it all in. Pure being, no thoughts, part of it all—the reason I came in the first place.

I don't know how long I sat like that before my gaze fell upon the buck. He must have walked out from behind the brushy spot. He appeared as en-igmatically and silently as every deer seems to—like a ghost ship in the fog, suddenly it is just there. He was just fifty feet in front of me. I hadn't moved but he looked directly at me, as aware of me as I was of him. I slowly eased forward to pick up the rifle, and he just as slowly eased away.

He was forty yards away before I dared to put the scope on him and then I had to wait for him to move between brush and trees. Quartering away, he looked back, giving me just enough angle. I squeezed off the round. What until now had been a complete hold-your-breath kind of silence, was ripped apart by the loud report of the rifle. The buck startled and looked back over its shoulder, right at me, for a long moment, before picking up his gait and moving away, again cloaked by trees and brush. But his walk was different: there was a hitch in it. I had hit him … not the kind of fatal shot that causes a panicked run, but a mere graze, likely in the hind sides, that I had tried so hard to avoid.

I looked for the chance of another shot. At one hundred and twenty yards, he was about to pass over the top of a knoll and out of sight. My hopes sank like the air out of a balloon. But, then he stopped. He stopped and turned to take one last look at me. There was little time, so I put the scope on him and fired. A ruckus erupted on the hill. In the confusion, I saw what looked like rolling, tail flagging, and leaves flying all at once.

I knew I had hit him! But, had he then bounded down the backside of the hill, fifty yards and into the neighbor's property? I waited. Two or three minutes passed. Then, I heard a shot just beyond where he had disappeared. Had the neighbor finished him? Must have … no sense in waiting now. Rifle in hand, I walked to the top of the knoll to examine the ground.

There I saw disturbed leaves and bare earth. And there it was, a puddle of blood the size of a paper plate. I looked ten yards further and there was another puddle, like the first, bright and crimson. Ten more yards … and to my amazement, there was the buck, down on all fours, blood flowing from a wound in his back just behind his shoulders.

There is nothing pretty about killing an animal. He was still alive, un-able to move, and looking directly at me. Our eyes met, with a kind of sadness and resignation that we each had for our parts in the drama of life. I silently thanked him and the Great Spirit for his sacrifice. I put the final shot in his neck and it was over. It is part of the great mystery that we live by eating other living things. I made no celebration but felt a humbling grate-fulness for the animal and to be part of it all.

At noon we had three deer hanging on the game pole outside the cabin. My eight-pointer dwarfed the other two. I won't say how small the Flick brothers' deer were, but if they had been shot just a month earlier they'd have had spots.

"Boy, the rookie shot a big buck!" said Bill.

"A really big deer," said Ducker. "I think the biggest one ever shot on our property!"

"About how many have been shot here?" I asked.

"About a hundred, I'd say," said Ducker. "Yeah, at least a hundred."

"Best deer out of a hundred," said Bill. "Now that's somethun! Dad would have been pleased that it was taken with his rifle."

"And Uncle Bob from his blind," added Ducker. "Good thing I sent the rookie over there."

I wondered if I'd get any of the credit!

Then, Bill cooked another fine meal and Dan and I tidied the camp. Talk of the big deer and recollections of hunts with Dad and Uncle Bob continued through the afternoon and into the night.

The next morning found me back in Uncle Bob's blind and Ducker just two hundred yards to my right in his rifle blind, the one I didn't find the day before. He couldn't resist the temptation of hunting near where the big deer had been taken, and I, satisfied and content, didn't mind the competition. I sat there in the warm glow of yesterday's unexpected good fortune. With the big buck already bagged, I truly expected nothing more. I went about the motions of hunting, sitting quietly, carefully setting the rifle in the corner of the blind, and maintaining a lookout. Soon the forest was awash in bright sunlight, and woodland creatures cautiously appeared and went about their daily business. As I sat there in the morning stillness, I thought about how lucky and yet undeserving I was of that big buck. I had prepared so little. Unlike all the other hunters in the woods, who had wanted one so much, I had just been there for the outing. Bill would have liked that deer, and yet he was so gracious in complimenting me. It is a big person who can take joy in the accomplishment of another.

Then, suddenly breaking my reverie came a ruckus of breaking branches and loud tramping. I turned to see three deer running from almost the exact spot where I had downed the big buck. A late-arriving neighbor must have frightened them. A big doe at full throttle led two smaller yearlings. As they came in range, I briefly wondered if you were supposed to shoot at a running deer. Why not, I concluded. And filled with confidence from yesterday's kill, I raised the rifle, tracked the big doe, and shot. She suddenly jerked, changed direction a bit, and ran on towards Ducker's rifle blind. A moment later I heard two shots. A couple minutes passed and Ducker's voice crackled on the walkie-talkie. "Rookie, get here quick, the neighbors behind me dropped the two little deer but said the doe just fell in front of them!" I arrived to find Ducker and two other hunters examining the doe. She was down, dead, with a shot in the heart, that, from the angle of it, only I could have made!

As we raised the doe on the pole next to the big buck and the two yearlings, Bill said, "Look, the two biggest deer were taken by the rookie!"

I laughed and said, "Enough of this 'rookie' crap, from now on call me 'Deadeye!'"

# A FISHING LEGEND AND THE WORLD WIDE WEB

Rusty Gates is a fishing legend. From his boyhood on the river to his running the family's Gates Au Sable Lodge, his expertise was unparalleled. He was a giant in conservation, the only president of the 900-member Anglers of the Au Sable. He was once selected Angler of the Year by *Fly Rod & Reel* magazine.

Who can argue with a best fisherman of the year? The only "best of year" I ever won was when one of my daughters brought home a tracing of her hand with the caption "to the best daddy of the year." I wondered who she gave it to the next year.

Then I caught and photographed a twenty-two-inch, bright-yellow brown trout, just one bend below Rusty's lodge. I took the photo of the fish and me into the lodge and showed Rusty. He got excited, gave me a pin, and entered my name in the Big Fish Log. Then he posted the photo on the lodge's website. I was thrilled … I was making a name for myself … I was honored. I called and emailed everyone I knew and directed them to my photo on the web. Several times that day, I visited the site and reveled in the glory of it. I did the same the next day. I thought my photo would surely remain for the week, perhaps a month, maybe the entire season. Then early in the morning on the third day, I logged on ... and there, to my surprise, was not my picture, but one of another trout, a bigger one, held by none other than Rusty's brother.

# A FIFTY GRAYLING DAY

"How many is that, Archer?" asked Bald Eagle.

"Forty-nine."

"What are you catching 'em on?"

"A number fourteen olive stimulator. They have all come on the same fly," I said. "If I can catch one more, I'll retire the fly and put it in a nice glass case and display it. This is my best day of fishing ever!"

We were fishing a lake in Yellowstone Park on our annual Venerable Fly Tyers trip west. We usually didn't bother with lakes—the streams being so good. But recent rains had our favorites high and muddy.

The trail in was some three miles. It undulated and meandered but was well marked and a pleasant hike in shorts and T-shirts. Near a big rock, we had to wait for a buffalo that stood facing us on the trail. We held our ground and soon it moved off to browse on tall grasses nearby. As we continued, it kept an eye on us and we on it.

Where the trail hit the lake, on the southeast shore, I stopped while my buddies walked on and began to spread out. I had seen something in that southeast corner that made me eager to fish it. I saw what looked like fins breaking the choppy water surface just beyond a growth of water lilies. I had never seen this before but had my suspicions. So, I edged into the lake and slowly waded through the thick water lilies. I was stopped just three feet short of their deepwater edge. There I stood on tiptoes with water an inch from the top of my chest waders. With elbows held high, I made my first cast to the cruisers in the water twenty feet beyond. Almost instantly, I hooked a fish. But as I brought it through the lilies, it tangled and I lost it. I tied on a new fly and cast again—another hit and hookup. This time I brought it to the edge of the lilies, then lifted and popped it up onto the disc-like surface of lily pads and brought it to my hand. It was a twelve-inch grayling.

I had never caught a grayling before so I took a long minute to look it over. I was struck by its beauty—light brown in color with iridescent shades of lavender, rose, and blue dancing on its tiny scales. The dorsal fin stood tall and proud and was clearly what I saw from shore. Its tail was deeply forked and on the other end it looked at me through a large eye. I put my nose to it and smelled the faint fragrance of thyme from which it gets its Latin name, *Thymallus arcticus*. Then its tiny mouth gulped at air, reminding me to slide it back into the water. With wonder, I watched it swim off.

I checked my tippet and fly, the stimulator, then cast it out among several more grayling, their tall sails breaking the surface and giving away their location. Almost instantly, I was hooked into another fish, retrieving it in the same manner as the last by popping it up on lily pads and skidding it over to me—what fun! The action was steady for the next half hour. I don't think a single cast went unchallenged. After about twenty fish, there were no more fins cutting the water and no more takers. I think that I had hooked them all.

I retreated a few feet back towards shore to a more comfortable depth. As I waited for more fish to show, I thought about the grayling that had once roamed my home waters, Michigan's Au Sable River. Like these fish, they had been too easy to catch and that contributed to their demise, although the story is a bit more complicated than that.

R. S. Babbitt came to the Au Sable in 1873, to survey the route for the Jackson, Lansing and Saginaw Railroad, which would run from Bay City to Gaylord. The railroad platted forty acres for a depot and a town at the site of an ancient Indian portage to the nearby Manistee River and named it "Crawford Station," after a Revolutionary War hero. There were no trout in the Au Sable then, but it abounded with a fish not known to the townsfolk. Babbitt took some of the strange fish to Bay City where fish enthusiast Daniel Fitzhugh identified them as a species of grayling, *Thymallus tricolor*. When Babbitt returned, a meeting was held in the railroad depot and the excited citizens changed the town's name to "Grayling."

Soon after, Daniel Fitzhugh introduced Au Sable grayling fishing to several of the nation's fish culturists and luminaries, including Fred Mather, Seth Green, Thaddeus Norris, and Charles Hallock. In Hallock's 1873 premier issue of the sporting periodical *Forest and Stream*, he extolled the Au Sable grayling and continued to do so numerous times in succeeding issues. The Au Sable grayling fishery was launched.

Fishermen flocked to the town on the new railroad. Trails were blazed along the river's banks. River lodges were constructed and local lads served as transporters and guides. The grayling were easy to catch and thus fished hard for the next thirty years. A sports fisherman could catch a hundred a day, and commercial fishermen put thousands on ice and exported them to big city markets in Detroit and Chicago.

Eventually, fishing pressure took its toll, but other factors also played in the extinction of the Au Sable grayling. The town of Grayling was then the epicenter of an extensive logging industry. Huge tracts of four-hundred-year old, two-hundred-feet tall white pines were cut down. None were spared, including those that shaded the river. Winter thaws and spring rains washed heavy loads of sand from the cutover through eroded banks into the stream. Logging drives scrubbed the river bottom and removed shoreside sweepers. Spawning gravel was scoured by those spring drives and then covered by sand. The assault on the grayling continued with the 1880s planting of brown trout and rainbow. By 1895, grayling were rare. The last one was seen in the neighboring Manistee River in 1897. The last remembered Au Sable grayling was caught in 1908 by guide Daniel Stephan. In the mid-1930s, the more remote Upper Peninsula stream, Otter Creek, yielded Michigan's last grayling. Gone was an entire subspecies of Arctic grayling unique to Michigan.

The grayling of Montana and Yellowstone Park, *Thymallus montanus*, is thought to be the parent strain of the Michigan grayling. Ten thousand years ago as the last glaciers retreated, grayling from Montana migrated to the Great Lakes. They remained as the earth rebounded from the glacial retreat. Both the Montana and Michigan strains became isolated pockets of grayling, separated from each other and from the parent species by hundreds of miles and thousands of years. Montana biologists, fortunate to have observed Michigan's loss, better protected their grayling and maintained good numbers of fish.

That history was not lost on me that day in Yellowstone, as I caught grayling after grayling. I saw no more fish in my spot among the lilies, so I exited the water and walked the lake's deadfall-laden banks to where other members of the Venerable Fly Tyers were catching rainbow trout. As I approached my friends, I noticed fins breaking the surface near the lake's outlet. No one was fishing to them, so I waded out as far as I could and cast my stimulator to the nearest rising fish. Wahmo—grayling. In the span of just two hours, I had gone from having never seen a grayling to being an expert at catching them, a dubious accomplishment considering how gullible they are. About then Bald Eagle wandered over and waded out into the water near me.

"Yes, forty-nine fish on one fly, that is amazing," said Bald Eagle.

I smiled and cast again, confident that I would achieve my "fifty-fish-on-one-fly feat" and that I would do it in front of a witness, none other than Bald Eagle, the Fishmaster himself. My fly hit the water, floated upright, a fin appeared a few feet from it, and swam towards it. The grayling's head emerged, its little mouth opened, and it swallowed the fly. I set the hook … and … it was gone! I reeled in my line and was crestfallen to see a curly end of tippet where the fly should have been.

"Tie on another size fourteen olive stimulator and catch number fifty with it!" said Bald Eagle. "It might not be the same fly, but it is the *same* fly."

And, so I did.

The next day, Bald Eagle, Moyski, and I set out to fish a small headwater stream that we hoped had cleared. This stream also related back to our Michigan home waters. It was a brook trout stream. It might seem silly to fish a stream that abounds in a fish that you can catch every day back home, but this water is special—and will remain unnamed—for it holds many more fish per acre than any I have fished anywhere. It also holds many ten-inch brookies, fine fish for a meal and is the main reason we fish it. Although we are normally catch-and-release fishermen, the Park wants brook trout removed, so we fish this once a trip and do not feel guilty about taking a meal from it.

After the grayling were extirpated from the Au Sable, the stream became a world-class brook trout stream. Rube Babbitt, the son of R. S. Babbitt, made a small planting of brook trout from the nearby Jordan River into the Au Sable's East Branch in 1890. With the grayling gone and the water slightly warmed by logging, brook trout populations soared. Because they were fall spawners, they were less affected by the log drives than the spring-spawning grayling had been. Soon the Au Sable was proclaimed by conservationist William B. Mershon to be "the most wonderful trout stream in the world," and again fishermen flocked to its fabled waters. With a size limit of eight inches and creel limit of fifty, brook trout became the second great Au Sable fishery.

The Au Sable's brook trout gained in reputation, not because they were large, but because they were plentiful and, like the grayling, easy to catch and delicious to eat. Soon a nationwide demand for them developed. While rainbows were shipped east, brook trout were shipped west.

Back to our no-name creek—it is small. So narrow that you can jump across it. It would be impossible to fish except that long stretches are in open country relatively free of shrubs and brush. It is best fished by kneeling on the bank and making long upstream casts. Any dry fly will do, but I am partial to the Royal Trude. The peacock herl and red floss body attract undiscriminating brookies, and the white wing makes it is easy to see.

I am particularly fond of fishing this stream and make it a highlight of every Yellowstone trip. I fish it with a six-foot-three-inch bamboo fly rod that I made to a Paul Young taper that he called the "Midge." It is just right for small fish in tight quarters.

Our creek is in grizzly country and we frequently find the bones of bison kills there. On one trip, I fished it with fellow Tyer, Ron Elzerman, a six-foot-four-inch-tall, two-hundred-and-fifty-pound giant of a man. I remember kneeling in the creek and casting upstream. The quiet water near me began to ripple and then I felt a thump-thump in the earth around me. I thought that I had either mistakenly entered the T-Rex pad of Jurassic Park or more likely a grizzly was nearing. I stole a frightened peek over my shoulder to see ... Ron Elzerman.

That day, as always, we caught many fish. Moyski was Fishmaster with a forty-seven fish total. Bald Eagle and I did not lag far behind. We carried out a stringer of fifteen brook trout of ten to eleven inches to feed six hungry Venerable Fly Tyers. Member Gary Marquardt, a professional chef, would cook them up for a memorable feast.

Walking the dusty trail back at the end of the day put Bald Eagle in a pensive mood. He looked at me and said, "You know, Archer, fly fishing isn't a matter of life and death, it is more important than that."

"How can that be?" I asked.

"Because if all we ever did was attend to life and death, in other words merely survive, there would be no time for art, no music, no dance, no recreation, and no fly fishing," said Bald Eagle. "Think how mean and base life would be then. No, life and death is just the foundation that allows us to have higher forms of human expression. Fly fishing, being one of those things, brings us such joy ... truly it is more important than that."

It made sense, and as we walked on, I gave it a lot of thought. Later, as Bald Eagle stretched his long legs and pulled ahead of us, I walked side by side with Moyski. I wanted to express to him just what Bald Eagle said to me. So, I said, "You know Moyski, fly fishing isn't a matter of life and death, it is more important than that."

"How can that be?" he said.

I stammered, and the words I needed, the elegant words of Bald Eagle, suddenly escaped me, so I said, "It just is!"

# JIMMY BUFFET, IF YOU READ THIS

I would like to be your copilot. We have a lot in common. I know something about aviation—see story one. I have purchased your records ... the best of Jimmy Buffet anyway. I too live in a house filled with women—see story four.

I promise not to be a hero worshipper—you must tire of that, Your Majesty!

# THE MOUSE THAT ROARED

"A bear that enters your tent does not have good intentions," the members of the Venerable Fly Tyers sang out in unison. Six of us, crammed into the media room of the Tower Ranger Station, were viewing the mandatory video required to receive a backcountry camping permit for the Third Meadow of Slough Creek. It was our fifteenth trip to Yellowstone National Park, and we had this briefing memorized. "If you encounter a bear, hold your ground, do not run!" again we chorused.

Ranger Bill, tired of us, cut the video and handed us the permit. Off we scampered to the campground parking lot at the base of the trail leading to the world-renowned Slough Creek. With fifty-pound packs, T-shirts, and bare legs, we embraced the forty-degree temperature of a high country early morning, knowing that it would soon be seventy degrees and full sun and we'd be hot from exertion.

The rock and scree trail to the Third Meadow is nine miles long and uphill—both ways! How can that be, you wonder? It undulates so much that it seems to be mostly uphill, or at least those are the parts you struggle with and remember. But the first section, the first mile going in, truly is uphill, with a four-hundred-foot altitude change. It starts with a hard climb, made harder because you haven't yet gotten your wind, or settled into your pace, or adjusted to the weight of your pack. The Venerable Fly Tyers call this part "Hellman Hill," after our own Dave Hellman, a big, powerful man, who in his younger days could have made easy work of the hill. But by the time he made his first trip, he was middle-aged, forty pounds heavier, and carrying a seventy-pound pack that actually included a portable shower. It almost killed him. The Venerable Fly Tyers, with a leave-no-one-behind policy, divvied up his stuff, ditched the shower, and assisted him to the top. Subsequent trips were never a problem for him, but the name "Hellman Hill" stuck like wet buffalo dung.

On this trip, we charged up the hill, with a "get it over with" kind of attitude. Soon we were laboring along, stretching out a bit, and then getting back together during frequent rest breaks. Forty-five minutes later, we finally reached the top and took a last, long break. A strong scent of sage and pine wafted through the air. A moose grazed nearby in a high, wet meadow. We cautiously passed it—it hardly noticed. Then a short downhill run took us to the near bend of Slough Creek, where we watched a few small fish rise to hatching midges. The water in this section is slow with switchback bends through the mile-wide open meadow. This is the First Meadow. Many fishermen stop and work this water—too many to our liking. As usual, we decided to move on to the less contested waters above and continued on the trail through a long series of ups and downs. We had found our pace, the trail widened, and we walked on two by two, chatting as we went. On uphill stretches, when exertion precluded talking, the sound of the bear bells that hung from our packs tinkled out the cadence. Soon we passed a rustic log cabin where backcountry rangers could stay and shelter their horses in barns, safe from the many bears that roam this corner of the park.

After another hour on the trail, we passed the cutoff to the Second Meadow. The river was a half mile off to our left and just above the narrow canyon between the first two meadows. In past years, we took that cutoff and camped at the Second Meadow, where we always enjoyed good fishing. But one year, we couldn't get a permit and instead had to take a campsite in the Third Meadow. That proved to be a stroke of great fortune.

Now, the Third Meadow is our annual destination. Camping is pleasant on its narrow, sloping sides. The creek's tighter bends and less water concentrate the fish, mostly sixteen- to eighteen-inch Yellowstone cutthroat. Best of all, the tougher, longer hike discourages the day fishers, and usually we are the only ones there.

I love the trail to the Third Meadow. It is long and hard, but there truly is a pot of gold at the end: the gold-colored Yellowstone cutthroat trout. The view along the way is a spectacular panorama of wide-open, grassy meadows, with forested high ridges on both sides. Slough Creek ribbons and meanders through the valley below. Narrow, cold feeder streams cross our path, carrying meltwater from the high ridges. Breeding geese and sandhill cranes emit raucous honks and calls that break the still air. We find shady rest spots in the few pine groves that cross the trail or from behind the occasional large boulder.

We trekked on, past where the stream diverged from the trail and edged back to the west, then around a high hill that defined the valley's wall and took us closer to the water again. A second ranger cabin came into view, constructed like the first and marking the bottom of the Third Meadow.

The Silver Tip Ranch, four miles farther, is the upper limit of the meadow. It is just above the park's northern boundary but requires the park trail for access. This ranch was built on land homesteaded in 1913 by a man named Milton Ames. In 1923, industrialist J. P. Morgan bought it and constructed the buildings that are here today, and it has remained in the hands of the very wealthy ever since. Sometimes we encounter wagons from the ranch traveling the park trail for supplies. The only other way in is by helicopter, which is reserved for the ranch's affluent guests. The wagons are pulled by horses and driven by working cowboys, fit men in worn chaps and jeans, with faded plaid shirts and large western hats with visible sweat rings. We exchange nods and move along.

We continued on for another two miles, the valley ever narrowing, until we came upon the cutoff trail marker, labeled 2S6. This is wild, open country, yet the few campsites scattered along the trail are strictly designated. They are set up with fire pits and bear poles to protect the campers and their food from the many black bear and grizzlies that frequent the area. The only things missing are picnic tables and outhouses—thank God! Because this is a particularly heavy grizzly area, a reported sighting can cancel your backcountry permit. That happened to us a couple of years ago. But this year ... this year we own Camp 2S6 for four days and three nights.

Bald Eagle took the narrow cutoff, and the rest of us followed single file. We climbed steadily for a hundred yards or so to a plateau about one hundred feet above the valley below. We found the fire pit of our designated campsite and wearily dropped the packs from our sweat-laden backs. We sat on logs and rested a bit before we removed our food items, bagged them, and hoisted them to the top of the bear pole. Next, we divided into two-man teams, found a spot of level ground, and set up our tents. Bald Eagle and I shared. I had carried the tent and ground cloth, he the water filter and cooking kit—lighter packs that way.

When the camp chores were finished, we donned our waders and bear spray, jointed our fly rods, and made for the river. Tall grass and clumps of bushes impeded our progress and prompted us to call out, "Here bear, here bear," just to be sure.

At the river's edge, we eased down an earthy, eroded bank. The stream there was twenty to thirty feet wide with a classic riffle-pool configuration, repeated every hundred yards or so. The water was the color of champagne, just six inches deep in the riffles and three to four feet in the bend pools, where the fish concentrated.

Bald Eagle decided to fish a slot where two shallow riffles formed a deeper, faster cut before hitting the bank pool. He tied on a parachute hopper and began deliberately plying the water. I watched him for a bit to see how the "Fishmaster" worked the stream. He reminded me of a heron, slowly moving into position, crouching low, and easing his beak forward to follow the drift. The ability to remain unseen cannot be overemphasized to the novice fly-fisher and is rarely taught by guides and fishing schools. The best fishermen, those who catch the most fish, are the stealthiest.

After Bald Eagle landed his second fish, I decided to move on. I was already down two to him and hadn't even started. Although I seldom do, I like to outfish Bald Eagle and spotting him two fish is not the way to do it. He says, "Fishing is not a competition, as long as I am catching the most." Well, he usually does.

I moved upstream to the next bend. In the tailout, I saw a good fish tight to the grassy bank, gently sipping something too small for me to see. I watched a bit, to take the measure of the fish and find its rhythm. It didn't move off that bank more than three inches; its rises were unhurried and delicate. It was a tough lie, and I knew only patience and accuracy would take this fish, so I slowly and carefully positioned myself twenty feet below and tied two feet of 6x tippet to the end of my leader and to that a size-20 parachute ant. My first cast was four feet above and a foot off the bank—not bad, but not good enough. I let the fly drift well beyond my target before quietly picking up. The next cast was six inches off the bank, then four, then just one inch off the grass. I held my breath as it slowly drifted to my fish. The take was gentle and only a slight raise of the rod tip was necessary to drive the small hook home. The fish swirled, then dove to the bottom to bulldog a fight there. Applying pressure as I could, I soon had it tired, then raised it to the surface and slid it into my net. The cutthroat was eighteen inches long and a deep golden brown, as if suntanned from sitting high in the water all day. I took a quick photo of it alongside my rod, my bamboo Phantom, then carefully revived the fish and released it for another fisherman on another day.

Fishing here is a joy and you can cover it all with a very small fly box. In fact, the hopper/ant combo is often all you need—in the upper meadows of Slough Creek, that is. It is another story in the other streams and rivers of the park. I once put together a list of flies for a new member's first trip to the park. I based it on the "Best Fly" of the day from my Yellowstone fishing journal. I rank ordered them and tallied the days that they prevailed:

| Stimulator | #14-16 | Yellow, Olive, Opal | 20 |
|---|---|---|---|
| Little Brown Trout | #6 | | 15 |
| Hopper | #8-12 | Bowleg Yellow, Olive | 12 |
| Bottom Scratcher | #10 | | 10 |
| Parachute Ant | #12, 18 | Black | 8 |
| Olive Sparkle Dun | #20-24 | | 8 |
| Royal Wulff/Trude | #14 | | 8 |
| Green Drake Sparkle Dun | #10-12 | | 6 |
| Better Beetle | #10, 12 | | 5 |
| RS2 | #20 | | 5 |
| Parachute Adams | #16, 20 | | 5 |
| Cicada | #10 | | 5 |
| Compara Emerger | #16, 20 | Tan, Olive | 4 |

| Elk Hair Caddis | #16 | Olive | 3 |
|---|---|---|---|
| Olive Flashback Nymph | #18, 20 | | 2 |
| Grouse & Herl | #18 | Yellow thread | 2 |
| BH Pheasant Tail | #18 | | 1 |
| WD40 | #20 | Gray | 1 |
| Rusty Spinner | #20 | | 1 |
| Telico Nymph | #10 | | 1 |
| Matuka | #6 | | 1 |
| Llama | #10 | Red | 1 |

If you add up all the days, you can see how blessed I have been to fish so many in the park. You can also see that the list is a pretty good mix of dry flies, nymphs, and streamers. For many years, we never fished streamers or nymphs because the action on dry flies was so good. But a few years back, we had a thirty-knot-wind day on the Third Meadow. You couldn't fish a dry fly … you couldn't cast it … you couldn't drift it. I put on my Little Brown Trout streamer that works so well in Michigan waters and had a phenomenal day. Others tried nymphs and they too did well. That day expanded our repertoire and virtually eliminated the occasional fishless day.

Back on the stream, I went on to catch many more fish that day, but the first was the most memorable. There is always a most memorable fish, and I carefully record it and the circumstances of its capture in my journal. As I crossed paths with my five buddies, they all reported having a great day on the water. We had roamed much of the four miles of the Third Meadow before the sun dropped behind the western ridge. Having worked back to the water near our camp, we stripped down and bathed in the waning light of the evening. In the brisk water, we happily laughed at our old, wrinkled bodies.

Renewed and invigorated, we hiked the short distance up the slope to our camp. Moyski and I gathered wood and built a fire. Bald Eagle and Hellman filtered water and replenished vessels drained from the hike and the fishing. Tobias and Viking set up the dining area. Soon six small pots danced on the fire's edge with a roiling boil of water.

The Venerable Fly Tyers make a ritual of reading the ingredients of their freeze-dried meals and debating the virtues of chicken cacciatore versus beef stroganoff or some other backwoods delicacy named by Marmot or REI. Though somewhat low in calories, the taste is excellent after long hours on the trail.

After dinner, we cleaned dishes and packed the trash to carry out on the return trip. Moyski put a few more logs on the fire and we gathered around. Six good friends talked of the hike and the fishing. Viking, a strong, powerful backwoodsman, encouraged everyone to push further, fish unexplored waters, and day hike above the Silver Tip Ranch to the Fourth Meadow. He told the tale of "Frenchy" Duret, a guide and friend of Theodore Roosevelt. Duret built a cabin in a nearby upper meadow, today known as "Frenchy's Meadow." On June 12, 1922, Frenchy inadvertently caught a grizzly in one of his traps. He shot the bear, but the wounded and enraged animal broke the chain holding the trap. Pieces of grizzly fur, strands of hair, torn bits of flesh, the blood-soaked ground, and chewed rifle stock all bore mute testimony to the struggle that had ensued. Two days later, park rangers found Frenchy's body and buried him there in the high country, near his cabin, to where he had crawled nearly a mile and a half before dying.

After that bear tale, Bald Eagle took it upon himself to give the Venerable Fly Tyers a review of backcountry bear safety procedures. With almost religious fervor, he rose to emphasize his theme. Meanwhile, Moyski and I saw a small mouse dart to the front of the fire. Unbelievably, it stood up on its hind legs, human-like, to warm itself, and looked to be listening to the ongoing diatribe. Just as Bald Eagle got to the part, "If you encounter a bear, stand your ground, don't run!" he stomped his foot for effect. This startled the poor mouse. It turned and ran right towards him, squeaking all the way. Bald Eagle let out a scream, jumped, and staggered two or three steps backwards before falling over the perimeter logs. Unhurt, he rose and brushed the dust off his jeans, while we all hooted. Then, Moyski asked, "How will he hold his ground in front of a bear, when he can't even hold it in front of a squeaky mouse?"

# HALF-DAY BUDDY

"You better practice your double haul, Archer! I have us all set up for a guided fishing trip to the Everglades," said Chuck. "I booked a guy named Buddy Ferber. Since it's our first time with him, I thought we'd just do a half day. He's new down here, so I don't know what we are getting into. I think a half day's best. Then if he's any good, we'll book him again. I wouldn't use a new guy except his rates are great, and he specializes in salt-water fly fishing and those guides are hard to find."

That conversation happened in January. Then in April, the big day came, and we were sitting outside Chuck's Florida home at six in the morning waiting for Buddy. A couple of minutes later, headlights turned onto Chuck's street. A big pickup pulling a seventeen-foot flats boat stopped in front of the house.

We sprang to our feet and rushed out to meet Buddy. The man grinning before us was about our age. He stood six feet tall with peppered black hair, graying at the temples. His skin was well tanned from long days in the sun. He was slim and he moved with the loose, fluid strides of Ray Bolger as the Scarecrow in *The Wizard of Oz*.

Buddy directed while we packed our gear in the boat, before getting in the pickup. The forty-five-minute ride to Chokoloskee gave us time to get acquainted. Buddy was new to South Florida, here because his mother was ill and needed care. He had come from Colorado, where he sold real estate and guided for trout.

Chokoloskee is a small island in a bay of the same name. It is located just south of Everglades City on Florida highway 29 and is a major gateway to the Everglades' salt-water sports fishing. At the Fishing Hole Boat Ramp, we unloaded Buddy's flats boat into the water and reorganized our gear for fishing.

As we slowly motored out into the harbor, a giant, red-orbed sun peaked over the cypress and mangroves of the Everglades. Mist lifted from the water, revealing a glass-smooth surface. Once clear of the harbor, Buddy opened the throttle and brought the Maverick flats boat up on plane. At thirty miles per hour, the chill forced Chuck and me to don jackets and zip them full up. We held on to our hats. We were flying through a maze of countless channels and islands as we headed south to Buddy's fishing grounds. How Buddy found his way, I have no idea; the low-lying mangrove-covered islands all looked the same to me. As we banked through each turn, I hoped to see no one coming the other way. I was exhilarated; this ride alone was worth Buddy's half-day fare.

The narrow channels between islands eventually opened to large lakes. Birds were active, and large flocks of terns, pelicans, white ibis, and flamingos filled the air. In some of the cuts, we disturbed alligators slumbering on mud flats. After about an hour, we left the inland waterway and ventured out into the Gulf. We slowed to a crawl about a half mile off Highland Beach and searched for tarpon. Several other boats were in the area, so it looked promising, and we saw a few of the big fish roll but none within casting range. Buddy didn't give it long, and soon we entered the Broad River and were blasting back deep into the glades. Occasionally Buddy would stop and one of us would get up on the deck and cast back into the mangroves.

We picked up fish this way: snapper, redfish, and snook. From the elevated platform on the back of the boat, Buddy was quick to see fish and get our eyes on them. Long casts were required to get deep into the mangrove roots. Buddy was patient with us and never complained about having to retrieve the flies that we frequently hooked on the vegetation. He only chided us if we weren't getting back there far enough. "That's where the fish are," he said.

It was Chuck's turn on the deck. Buddy saw a large snook in the mangroves and worked to get Chuck's eyes on it. A longer cast than we had been making was required. Chuck tried to power it to no avail, until Buddy explained that you can't add power to the forward stroke, but you can add it to the haul. On Chuck's next cast, he put the fly on the money and the big snook came out and inhaled it. Chuck worked hard to keep the fish out of the mangroves and soon had it to the boat. Buddy leaned over the side and secured the fish with a Boga Grip. He handed the subdued snook to Chuck, who held it high while I snapped the photo.

Watching Buddy work with Chuck, I saw a guide who went the extra mile to give his clients a great experience. He saw our weaknesses and found ways to fix them, all the while telling us what great fishermen we were. It was a balance that paid off, and we got better and better as the day progressed. As I watched Buddy, I thought about a story from my childhood and a guide who became a legend in my hometown.

I was born and raised in the town of Green Lake, on the lake of that name, in Wisconsin. For a brief period, my home lake became a fishing Mecca. It happened in the 1950s. The population of lake trout in the Great Lakes had crashed. They were decimated by the lamprey, which were let in by the 1932 completion of the Welland Canal. In less than two decades, the lamprey were everywhere and the lakers were gone. Midwest sports fishermen had lost a top-end fishery and began looking for a replacement. A careful review of stocking records revealed that Green Lake, two hundred and thirty-seven feet deep, the deepest in the state, had been stocked twice with lake trout some fifteen years earlier. Local fishermen never caught those fish due to the great depths at which they lived. Occasionally, a strange fish caught through winter ice was reported, but it went unidentified.

One summer, a retired army major vacationed on the lake. He had grown up in New York's Finger Lakes area and suspected that Green Lake's depths might hold lakers. He fished thin silver spoons off deepwater ledges and soon was catching fish. Some of the local bass and walleye guides got wind of this and began plying the deep water as well but without success. They simply did not know what gear to use. Polite queries to the major went unanswered. So, several guides in their boats converged on the major one day, catching him in the act of fishing, and were able to view his terminal tackle.

In the blink of an eye, Green Lake became the lake trout capital of the Midwest. Not only did the lake hold fish, they were thirty- to forty-pound lunkers, and they were plentiful. A dozen or more pontoon-rigged guide boats carried vacationing sportsmen from Chicago to Minneapolis out onto the lake for the big fish.

One of the nearby Green Bay television stations had a sports anchor by the name of Big Al Sampson. Big Al was all of five-feet-four-inches tall and weighed one hundred and thirty-five pounds. The only thing big about him, besides his oversized head, was his desire to catch fish.

One fine summer day, he and his legion of cameramen descended on Green Lake. One of the lake's finest, a certain Dee-Dee Carver, was his guide and sported a new pontoon boat, fully rigged for lake trout. After a couple of hours on the water, Big Al's rod took a deep bend. A great fish was on and Al worked it up and towards the boat. In his excitement and contrary to Dee-Dee's direction, he brought it up too quickly.

When the fish was beside the boat, Dee-Dee tried to net it. But he missed; the fish threw the lure and sank out of site. Dee-Dee, fully clothed, dove over the side of the boat. About ten feet down, invisible to those on deck, he found the fish, on its side, inert from a distended swim bladder that hadn't had time to adjust to its quick ascent. Dee-Dee quickly hooked a finger through the gill plate. He swam under the boat and then slowly and silently to the surface between the two pontoons and under the deck, where he silently remained.

Topside, Big Al and crew leaned over the railings and gazed down into the algae-laden water that gave the lake its name. They expected to see an empty-handed Dee-Dee emerge at any moment. That moment grew like the nose on a liar.

Big Al asked, "How long's he been down now?"

One of the cameramen said, "About two minutes I think." And they all looked at their watches, marking the time.

"Three minutes," was reported, then "four" and "five."

Big Al again: "How long can a man hold his breath anyway?"

No answer. Six minutes. Seven.

Sampson panicked. "God this is a disaster … stop the cameras … we are going to be involved in a drowning and likely a lawsuit as well!"

"Eight minutes" and "nine" were called before Dee-Dee, fish in tow, slipped back under the water, dove deep, and swam under the starboard pontoon. As "ten" was announced, a mighty scissors kick propelled him from the invisible depths, through the surface, fish held high at arm's length. He passed the fish to the eager hands of a cameraman, then fell back into the water, feigning exhaustion. It took two crew members to help him onto the deck of the boat.

As Dee-Dee lay there in the puddle from his soaked clothing, Big Al forgot all about him. Instead, he held and admired his fish and glammed for the cameras. Finally, in an afterthought, he looked down at Dee-Dee and said, "Carver, is this the same fish I hooked and you muffed on the net job?"

Dee-Dee looked up at him and with considerable mock effort said, "How would I know, Al? There are so many lake trout in Green Lake, I just swam down to the bottom and grabbed the nearest one I could find!"

Back in the Everglades, Buddy got the tarpon bug again and took us deep into the backwaters. We passed a campsite called Camp Lonesome. I quickly got out my cell phone, searched through my iTunes, and played Ricky Nelson's *Lonesome Town*. Buddy loved it and made me play it again and again as we drove through a half mile of tight mangroves that eventually opened onto a twenty-acre lake. This was Buddy's secret spot and he got out the big rods, the ten- and eleven-weights, and rigged them with a big fly pattern he called an EP Peanut in black and purple.

I was up and working the mangroves to my left as Buddy poled the boat. He had me retrieve the fly farther in than usual. Soon, when my fly was close to the boat, and I was just about to pick it up, I saw the blur of a large fish streak at it and then felt a hard hit. Line screamed off my reel and in a heartbeat, fifty feet ahead, five feet of silver came out of the water, apexed, rolled, and knifed straight back down.

"Point the rod at it, point the rod at it!" shouted Buddy.

I did and the hook held. A hundred feet out, the tarpon breached again. I pointed at it and again it held. I was hooked to a rocket ship, and already it was deep into my backing. Then the fish made a hard left towards the mangroves. I gained some line at first and tried to pressure it out of there, but it was hopeless. We could hear it crashing through the mangroves and occasionally leaping over roots as it reversed course and headed back our way. Soon, my line was hopelessly tangled and the big fish gone.

We were silent for a long time, trying to take in all that we had just seen. I slowly coaxed my line out of the tangles and back onto the reel. This was the largest fish of our day so far and the largest that I have ever had at the end of my line. It took several moments to get over losing that fish.

Reluctantly, I relinquished the deck to Chuck. He no more than got up on top and began to strip out line for his first cast, when another tarpon rolled not twenty feet in front of us.

"Cast Chuck, cast!" Buddy and I yelled together.

In a hurry, he made an awkward cast that landed behind the fish. He quickly picked up and cast again, and we held our breaths … and then all hell broke loose. The fish took the Peanut fly and was off to the races. It jumped once, and we saw it was huge and much bigger than mine. Chuck played it well, kept the rod tip low, often in the water in an effort to keep the fish from leaping. It worked—the fish never jumped again, only rolled and porpoised several times. It towed our boat like a truck commercial—or like a whaleboat harpooned to Moby Dick. Chuck had the drag on his reel clamped down hard, giving as little line as he could, relying on the weight of the boat to slow the fish.

Late in the fight, the drag on Chuck's reel burned out and it began to free spool. Fortunately, he managed to palm the reel's rim and maintain control of the fish. My God, he is a good fisherman! By the time it was done, the fight had lasted an hour and ten minutes and the boat was pulled, by my estimate, more than two miles. The lyrics of *Lonesome Town* rippled through the air as Chuck wound the leader through the rod's tip top and Buddy managed to bring the fish alongside the boat. Buddy estimated it to be more than seven feet long and weigh upwards of one hundred and twenty pounds. At that point, the giant tarpon made one more contortion, broke the leader, and slowly swam away. The four of us, three on the boat, and the one in the water, were all glad it was over.

Chuck looked exhausted and I was tired from just watching as we motored out of Buddy's lucky tarpon spot. We were deep in the Everglades and well south of Chokoloskee. A brisk wind forced us to take the calmer inland water route. As I again enjoyed the exhilarating ride, I thought back on the day and the experience with Buddy and concluded that Buddy just liked to fish—just liked to be out there. He wore no watch; he was a sun-to-sun kind of guy.

The boat ride back to the dock took almost two hours. After loading the boat on the trailer and the drive to Chuck's house, we got home at eight p.m., fourteen hours since our early morning pickup.

As Buddy retrieved our gear from his boat, Chuck and I met at the front of the pickup.

"That was some half day," I said.

"I guess to Buddy that means twelve hours on the water," said Chuck.

"How should we pay him?" I asked. "His half-day rate seems too low."

"We'll pay his half-day rate plus a generous tip to make it come to his full-day rate and a bit more," said Chuck.

As we gave Buddy his well-earned money, I said, "Buddy, that was an incredible day for a half day. We are wondering what we would get for a full day?"

Buddy winked and said, "The same. Perhaps you shouldn't tell anyone about my half-day deal!"

# THE LAST ROCK IN THE LAMAR

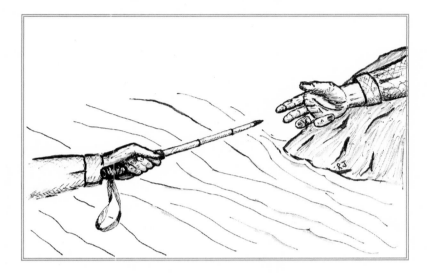

If Archimedes had a lever long enough and a place to stand on, he could have moved the world. The place to stand on is the trick!

We slid to a quick stop in the gravel pullout, then bounded out of the car, anxious to get on the river. No one else was there—a good omen that elicited a hearty high five. Dave Hellman and I donned our waders and boots while sitting on large rocks. Rods joined and reels seated, we trekked down the dusty trail that sits two hundred feet above the Yellowstone River off to our left. The trail hugs the edge although there is a large open plateau to the right with grasses, sage, and an occasional stunted tree. I suppose fishermen want to see the river so they walk the edge.

Along the trail, we caught glimpses of the Yellowstone's roiling waters, through gnarled, white-barked pines. The stunted trees eked a meager existence along a windy ridge of talus and rock. A red-tailed hawk circled above, hunting pikas and ground squirrels.

The bright morning sun lit the far canyon wall, producing contrasts of shadow and light. Even from our height, we heard the roar and felt the power of the surging river as it entered the Black Canyon of the Yellowstone. The gradient was steep, the water fast and powerful. Large rocks and boulders split the raging current. Piles of weathered timber were stacked like a giant pick-up sticks game where the spring spates had left them.

I remember another trip here. A cloud of small mayflies whirled above the fast waters. There were millions in a swirling cyclonic vortex rising from the river's surface to well above the high ridge sides. I wondered where on this torrent they settled to lay their eggs and if they were eaten by trout in invisible rise forms.

We continued along the Yellowstone until we reached the point where the Lamar joined from the east. The open plateau on our right gave way to its narrow valley of rock and ponderosa pine. Hellman chose to drop down to the confluence directly, while I turned right and followed the plateau up the Lamar. After a quarter mile, the drop to the river was easy. I only slipped twice on the scree and loose pine needles, falling on my backside and laughing at my haste to get to the stream.

I circled around the bank of a large back-eddied pool, then climbed atop a boulder that placed me eight feet above the water. From there I would be able to make long casts to both the pool and the hard flow at its edge. I watched for rising fish for several minutes, saw none, and thought, "It's going to be a streamer day."

From my Yellowstone fly box, I selected a Little Brown Trout. I tied it to three feet of 2x tippet and sinking tip line. The Little Brown Trout is my variation of Lefty Kreh's Deceiver pattern. It is effective and has become popular among my fellow Venerable Fly Tyers.

I can take credit only for the dressing. And like most things fly fishing, we stand on the backs of giants. Lefty's Deceiver is, in my opinion, the finest baitfish pattern ever devised—so hats off to you, Lefty! But you don't need me telling you that. After all, the U.S. Postal Service issued a stamp in your fly's honor.

My Little Brown Trout is dressed with yellow grizzly feathers beneath strands of fox squirrel hair, with a belly of yellow and then white calf tail and a red soft-feather throat. The head is dark olive thread, lacquered smooth and painted with white eyes and black pupils. Originally tied for Michigan waters, I called it the Little Brown Trout, while here in Yellowstone it could just as easily be called the Little Cutthroat Trout. I also have Little Rainbow and Little Brook Trout versions, but those are stories for another day.

I began casting into the quiet waters of the pool, first working the edge along the main flow, then the rocky bank edges, and finally the deepwater center. I thought I saw a flash there once but was not sure. I took no fish. I had taken fish there before, but on that day, the pool was as stingy as a Depression-era banker.

The Lamar is streaky and known for fish that can be found in one place today and another tomorrow. And, I am giving up no secrets to say we fished the Lamar. Every fisherman who comes to the park knows it. Most fish the waters near the road. A few, like the Venerable Fly Tyers, hike in to the hard-to-reach places. If you do, you better not be afraid of bear or bison, for they like those spots too.

I remember coming here once and seeing a sign at our usual pullout that said, "Area Closed Due to Bear Activity." We drove to the next pullout, then the next; five pullouts in a row had the same sign. The sixth and last pullout did not. So, we donned our gear and began the mile hike downhill to the river. Over the first crest, not more than one hundred yards in, we came across a bear kill: a small, partially eaten bison with bear sign all around. So, there was the kill … at the only pullout that wasn't closed!

Hellman broke the silence when he radioed, "Fish on, a twenty-incher, I need a witness." For a member to be eligible for the Venerable Fly Tyers' Big Fish Award, a witness is required. I was being called upon to perform that honorable task. I radioed back, attached the Little Brown Trout to my fly rod's hook keeper, and hurried towards him at the confluence below.

After quickly climbing over hundreds of rocks the size of tool chests, I was breathless when I came upon Hellman standing on the rocky shore, rod bent, connected to a good fish. But, it wasn't a twenty-incher, more like fifteen. Hellman tends to stretch the length of a fish … perhaps the reason for the Fly Tyers' witness requirement.

Soon he eased the tired fish out of the fast water, bent over, and released it in the slack current around the rocks. He smiled up at me a bit sheepishly and then held up, for me to see, the streamer that took it. Yes, it was a Little Brown Trout!

Hellman welcomed me, and we fished side by side in the fast water where these two great streams meet. It is an unusual confluence. The Lamar comes in perpendicular to a big outside bend of the larger river, and there it meets a raging wall of water. It is as if the Yellowstone doesn't want it to join. The turbulence there is violent, and one hundred yards below it crashes against rocks as the bend tightens. Two years ago, we came to this spot and weren't allowed to fish. A team of park rangers were dragging the water for the body of a summer-help college kid who drifted his inner tube a bit too far down the Lamar. To the horror of his onlooking, river-frolicking companions of macho males and bikini-clad girls, he was swept up by the Yellowstone, the tube flipped, and he dropped from sight forever.

Hellman was one of the founding members of the Venerable Fly Tyers. He is a six-foot-two, two-hundred-forty-pound, barrel-chested man. If the Venerable Fly Tyers were a hockey team, he'd be the enforcer—that is, if he didn't have such an affable disposition. Like many big men, he is rarely threatened and generally finds the world agreeable. He is quick to share in good things as he did that day when I joined him on his stretch of the Lamar.

The fish here are slim and twelve to fifteen inches long, not as large as those in the quieter water nearby. They find a bit of still water, deep and behind a large rock, and shoot up through the turbulent white water above for their food. Their takes are sudden and hard, and once hooked, the current magnifies their fighting ability—making a fifteen-incher feel like a twenty-incher, I suppose.

We fished side by side, carefully casting to avoid each other's fly and line. After Hellman collected eight fish, and I only three, things slowed. Every fish in our water had seen our folly and stopped chasing. I suppose we had taken all the players, or perhaps those hooked informed their buddies of the danger of the Little Brown Trout. Nevertheless, many empty casts caused us to look for other options.

The width of the Lamar and the limited room for backcasting kept us from reaching the water on the far side. With great effort, we could have moved upstream where the river is widest, carefully crossed, and then come back down. We have done that before. While considering that proposition … it was then that I saw the rock. It sat several feet off the bank in about five feet of fast-flowing water. In the clear water, I saw a submerged rock bridge that might let me carefully wade to it. The rock itself projected out of the water about two feet. It was round and the size of a coffee table, just right to stand on and cast to the far side.

At the edge of the bank, I carefully eased into the fast water. Waist deep, I secured each footfall on the underwater bridge before making another. One step, two steps, three, four, and I had my left hand on the rock. It was granite, not smoothed by eons of water wear, but rough as if it was recently placed there by a great spring spate. I swung my right shoulder and arm and placed my right hand, with fly rod, on the rock above my left … then my right knee and pulled my chest up onto the rock … left knee, then pushed up onto all fours. Then I stood.

For a moment all was well, but the water from my waders and boots drained onto the rock and made it slick. I balanced precariously, waving my arms unsteadily, tried to reposition my feet … and then slipped. Slowly at first, then gaining momentum as my feet slid out from under me. I was headed directly towards the torrent on the far side of the rock. Even when I dropped and pancaked myself to the rock, I continued to slide off its far curved edge. Time slowed; I debated letting go of my fly rod. I should have, I suppose, but just couldn't—I built it just for this trip, just for this spot. I continued to slide. I was flat to the rock and pressing myself into its roughness. My legs were now mid-thigh in the current, which twisted me farther off the rock and towards the Yellowstone. And then, my left index finger slid into a small depression … and held. My slide was stopped by one finger!

But, I still wasn't out of danger. I still had to pull myself back up onto the rock. I edged my right arm, with rod in grip, above the left and found a bit of a ridge. Slowly, I pulled myself back up the rock, my face and chest still buried in it. Inch by inch, I managed to get my feet out of the water and my belly on the apex. I rested there a bit before rising to all fours. There would be no second attempt to stand!

And where was Hellman, the enforcer, during all this? On the bank yelling, "Oh my God, oh my God!" In his defense, there was really nothing he could have done. He couldn't reach me and he couldn't have waded across the underwater bridge to me in time. Helplessly watching my near demise must have been harder on him than it was on me. After all, I at least had some control of the outcome.

Hellman leaned out at the river's edge, and I handed him my fly rod and took his wading staff. Then, I turned and eased myself into the quieter water on the inside of the flow. I worked along the submerged rock bridge back to the bank. Soon I was sitting next to Hellman on a couple of big rocks, well back from the water.

We were both breathing hard. I think Hellman was more frightened than I was. We sat there for a long time—me thinking how foolish I had been, and he imagining how he would have had to explain it to our buddies and the authorities.

As I sat there, what bothered me most was not the close call, but the fact that I took it without once thinking of the risk involved. Have I become so immune to risk? When a squadron commander gets the dreaded call that one of his planes has crashed, he has a fifty-fifty chance of guessing the pilot. It will be either his worst pilot or his best. The worst, for obvious reasons. But, the best—the best believes that the rules were not made for him and thus takes greater risks—that is partly why he is the best. But, a risk is a risk! It is not just a brief flirt with death—it gives death a real opportunity.

Bruce Lee, the great martial artist, once wrote, "Never enter a fight anticipating the outcome!" This may be a great axiom for combat and flying fighters but perhaps not for the old pilot turned fly-fisherman. I climbed out on that rock thinking only of the fish that I might catch, without once thinking of the risk. A humbler and wiser fisherman scabberred home that day!

# A THOUSAND-DUCK POTHOLE

"I've never seen so many ducks in my life," whispered Woody, as we kneeled at the edge of the pothole.

"Me neither. What are we going to do?" I whispered back.

Dan "Woody" Woodbury and I were squadron mates in the 25th Flying Training Squadron at Vance Air Force Base, near Enid, Oklahoma. He was five years my junior at the Air Force Academy. He was born and raised in Gunnison, Colorado, on the ranch settled by his maternal grandfather. He had enough Native American blood from both his parents to be considered a "legal" Indian. He learned to ride and rope at an early age. At the Academy he briefly played fullback/defensive back on the football team. But frustrated with college football, he quit and started the Academy's collegiate rodeo team. His father had flown F4U Corsairs with "Pappy" Boyington in WWII, and again in Korea, undoubtedly Woody's inspiration to become a pilot. He stood six feet tall, weighed two hundred pounds, and was tough and lean. He had curly dark hair and a handsome face, roughened by the outdoors. If he were an actor, he could have played either a cowboy or an Indian.

Woody introduced me to duck hunting. Four of us from the 25th Squadron—Mike Gipson, John Rogers, Woody, and I—hunted together on many fall weekends. We headed to the Canadian River, twenty miles west of base, and hunted the small lakes that one hundred and fifty years ago were buffalo wallows in the river's flood plain. Ducks from the Central Flyway navigated along the Canadian during their fall migration and settled into the nearby small lakes for shelter and to feed on milfoil, coontail, and duckweed.

Getting permission to hunt there went like this: We found the nearest ranch stead and knocked on the door. A lanky, grizzled old rancher answered. He was hesitant at first but then said, "Is it ducks? Ducks you wanna hunt? Go ahead, I got no use for 'em. But stay away from my frogs, ya hear!"

The next morning, we arrived early, set up in the dark, wind at our back from the south, and waited in the cattails for opening time, thirty minutes before sunrise. We enjoyed early action, mostly teal and redheads. Teal are straight shooters; like a reconnaissance pilot, they are alone, fast, and unarmed. They often hit the water in the middle of your decoys before you see them.

But redhead ducks are suicidal. They are easy to call and will swing right into your deeks without the circumspect circling of a mallard. Take three or four out of a dozen incomers, and the rest will fly out, regroup, and come right back in. And they will do that again and again until there is none left. Mallards won't do that, look-alike canvasbacks won't do that ... in fact, I have never seen another species of duck so intent on becoming table fare as the redhead.

After the early-morning action died down and quiet set over the marsh, we gathered the fallen ducks and settled back into the cattails. Slowly a bright, sunny sky emerged over the pond. It was deceiving because looming to the northwest was the leading edge of a front. It filled a quarter of the sky and was about ten miles away. The sun lit the big lead cloud well, and a dozen flights of ducks traveled back and forth across the luminous dome in the distance. We knew there would be more shooting. But it wasn't there yet, so we settled back into the cattails and waited.

I sat on a wooden seat, lit a pipe, and maintained surveillance over the marsh. I looked for the frogs the rancher said were there. In the dark mucky water, I saw one ... a whole foot long ... then another. My God, that rancher had something here and he was feasting on it; no wonder he was so protective. As I looked down for more frogs and up for ducks, I heard something odd. Faint at first, it became louder. It sounded like laughter. I tried to associate it with the frogs but that didn't work—frogs croak, not laugh. It got louder and sounded like children laughing. It was out of place in the marsh, so I decided to investigate. The laughter came from behind me, and I knew what was back there from an early retrieval of a duck—more cattails and in one spot a small opening.

I rose quietly and slowly worked my way back towards the sound. As I edged into the opening, I saw a strange sight. Two raccoons were catching huge tadpoles—they weren't just catching them, they were playing with them. Like the old hand-over-hand gripping of a baseball bat to decide the first batter, the raccoons faced each other, one took a tadpole in its hand and squeezed it out and up, the other reached in and did the same, until all four hands had squeezed and shot the tadpole well above their heads. Then one raccoon opened its mouth to catch and swallow the falling tadpole. They both laughed and did it again. I have never seen animal behavior so human-like, and I stood in awe at their fun and laughter. I didn't want to spoil their moment, so I respectfully turned and quietly slipped back into the cattails and returned to my spot in the marsh.

I wondered then and again today, as I write this: What were tadpoles doing in the marsh in October—they should have been frogs by then. I did a little research and learned that tadpoles stay in the juvenile form for a few weeks to two years, depending on the frog species. As big as this pond's frogs were, they must have been on the two-year plan.

An hour later, the wind changed as the front came upon us. When the first gust hit, we thought about switching around our position and decoys, but there were so many ducks in the air that we couldn't steal out and do it. It didn't matter. Soon ducks came in from every direction, our cannons blasted, and ducks fell. In half an hour, we finished our limits, ten each at that time. Then, as the first pellets of a wind-driven sleet fell upon us, we collected the decoys, and headed out a half step ahead of a cold, winter blast.

A week later, Woody and I were back along the Canadian, just the two of us this time and on a different pond. We embraced the chill of a morning hunt and set up our decoys as usual with a strong northern wind at our backs. As the sun rose, we had a flurry of early shooting, killed a duck each, and then settled into the usual morning lull. By nine a.m., there were clear skies and the ducks were flying high. None came into our spread or to our call. The loud highball call might get a look or two but no takers.

As we scanned the sky, a mile or so to our northwest, we saw many ducks circle, then disappear below the tree line. In fact, at times there were so many ducks that they literally swirled in their descent. It seemed to be a one-way trip—fly by, circle back, and disappear. And, they did not reappear. Whatever was attracting them, held them.

We were transfixed. We had to know what the draw to that spot was and how many ducks were there. Perhaps we could get permission to hunt it! So, we gathered our decoys, loaded the truck, and set out for the magic spot. It wasn't as close as we thought and took a few false turns in the mile-square grids of the Oklahoma road system to finally find our destination. There we found a large pine plantation with a two-track entrance and a prominent "NO TRESPASSING" sign attached to a steel ranch gate.

"Well, what would it hurt if we just took a look?" said Woody, and I readily agreed. We found the gate unlocked and with one set of eyes on the road, swung it open, drove through, and closed it behind.

We parked the truck a quarter mile in and at the far edge of the pines and got out. A bit of high ground blocked our view, but we could hear a cacophony of duck chatter. We cautiously walked on and soon saw a five-acre pond covered with ducks and with more funneling in. There were mallards, teal, widgeon, gadwall, pintail, redheads, canvasbacks, and heaven knows what else. It was like those *Ducks Unlimited* magazine photos captioned with, "How many different ducks do you see?"

What made this pond different from the others around it? We had no idea but knew we couldn't just pass it up. If there is such a thing as "duck fever," we had it and we had it bad. We quickly and stealthily returned to the truck, got our shotguns, loaded them, and snuck back to the pond. We agreed to flush a few of the closest ducks, pick one each, and shoot it. That's all—one each.

When we were in place and kneeling at the pond's edge, Woody jumped up and let out a "HO" and up they went. I selected a big drake mallard twenty yards out and two feet off the water, pulled lead, and shot. Our shots were simultaneous because Woody didn't hear mine and yelled, "Don't shoot, don't shoot!"

"Too late," I said, as we watched a thousand ducks take to the air, climb high into the sky, and fly off for safer waters. After watching the duck exodus in wonder, we lowered our eyes to the pond. Our jaws dropped as we saw what looked like the devastation of a tornado-hit Oklahoma town. There were dead and wounded ducks everywhere; there were huddled, still birds, a wing flapping here, an orange leg kicking there, a couple cowering swimmers heading for the pond's far side.

Despite aiming for just one, we had hit so many. Suddenly we realized that we were trespassing and shooting ducks on someone else's pond, and we nearly panicked. We had no idea where the owner might be. But the sound of our shots and a thousand flying ducks must have been discernible for miles. In addition to that, what about our duck limits? This was during the years of the point system, where each species counted towards one hundred points. Teals, widgeons, pintails, and gadwalls counted for ten points, but mallards, redheads, and canvasbacks were thirty- or forty-point ducks!

But this was no time for calculations ... or remorse; this was a time for action. We had to retrieve all those ducks and get out of there! So, over the course of the next half hour, with frequent over-the-shoulder glances, we waded into the pond and rounded up all the ducks we could easily pick up. Fortunately, the pond was shallow and the bottom firm. What about the cripples? We were nervous about shooting again, so we corralled the cripples between us and caught those we could by hand. Some we just couldn't catch, so we left them for the foxes and hawks that would pick them off later.

Back at the truck, we hurriedly stuffed the birds and our gear into the back and lit out like a rabbit ahead of hounds. We made it—no vehicles on the road, no sirens, and no angry ranchers. A few miles down the road, we pulled into a wayside and examined the spoils. We had ten ducks each; almost all were ten-pointers. Although one hundred points was the limit, you could exceed it with the last duck, so, amazingly, we were legal!

Of all the duck hunts before and since, I've never had another one like that. I say with remorse that it was the duck fever that made us do things we normally never would. And I wouldn't do it again ... but, oh my, there is nothing like hunting a thousand-duck pothole!

# WHAT KIND OF WHISKEY WAS THAT?

"I Want to Believe!" Doc Scott read out loud from the poster on the wall. The Venerable Fly Tyers had just crowded around a table in the Bearclaw Bakery for the best breakfast in Cooke City, Montana. Nothing could have described our mindset better than that statement from *The X-Files*. It was our first day in yet another trip to Yellowstone National Park. We "wanted to believe" that the fishing would be great!

Moments before, we had hustled down to the restaurant to beat the opening crowd. There are only four tables and arriving early was essential. Terri, the proprietor, was scurrying about the kitchen and smiled as she recognized us from years past. In one of those years, she opened the Bearclaw on her day off, so we could eat before beginning our trip home. It was a strange feeling eating breakfast that day, while others came to the door, found it locked, and were turned away. They peered through the window, wondering, "Who are *those* guys?" We felt like rock stars, and Terri earned our everlasting loyalty.

Over bacon and eggs, breakfast burritos, and French toast, we planned the day. This is more a negotiation than a discussion for the Venerable Fly Tyers. Everyone has his pet waters and favorite fishing partners. Because it was our first day, we wanted to stay together and so decided that Moyski and

I would fish from the Lamar Bridge down to Rainbow Alley. Meanwhile the rest of the crew would hike into Rainbow Alley and fish up to rendezvous with us. It was a good plan—with just one problem … we didn't know if it was possible. We had never fished that stretch all the way before and weren't sure the water or canyon walls would allow it, and there was Slough Creek to cross.

Breakfasts tucked into full bellies, we hiked up the loose gravel hill to our cabins at the Antlers Lodge. We've stayed at the Antlers for years now. We love the Old West feel of the aged log cabins. They were built in 1913, more than a hundred years ago, by the Shaw family. The lodge has changed hands several times through the years and now Kay and Bill Whittle own it. They made needed repairs to the old cabins and added several new, more spacious ones, while still maintaining the authentic atmosphere.

We hurriedly packed our gear, grabbed our fly rods, and set out for the day. The drive into the park is jaw-dropping gorgeous. Although we've made this trip many times, it has never lost its luster. The road winds through the tight Soda Butte valley with rapidly rising slopes on both sides. Mature lodgepole pine and Douglas fir line the valley from the edge of the road to the tree line. Glimpses of the creek reveal stands of quaking aspen and willow, coloring the river bottomland in shades of yellows and lime. We were only eight miles from Granite Peak in the Beartooth Range. At 12,807 feet, it is the tallest mountain in Montana.

We slowed to pass through the tiny town of Silver Gate. Fingers of scorched and burned trees approached the road along the northern slope. These were remnants of the Yellowstone fires of 1988. That conflagration of more than fifty individual fires burned almost 800,000 acres, more than a third of the park's forests. It had broken the boundary of the park to the east and narrowly missed the towns of Silver Gate and Cooke City.

Two minutes later, we stopped at the Northeast Park Entrance Station. We gained entrance with our Golden Passes. Then we pulled into a parking spot to purchase park fishing licenses. A congenial park ranger made the task easy, and soon we were on our way again. We motored into the park on the Northeast Entrance Road, U.S. Highway 212. As the road turned to the south, we crossed into Wyoming and entered the Absaroka Mountains. On our right, Barronette Peak commanded a long, high ridge of weathered sandstone columns. The road pullouts were filled with park visitors glassing for marmot, bighorn sheep, and mountain goats. There, the animals stand out against the pink, red, and tawny rocks.

Beyond the Barronettes, the valley widened and Soda Butte Creek braided. We crossed the Pebble Creek Bridge and saw a small bison herd grazing on rich bottomland grasses. Vehicles were parked on both sides of the road to watch. We once did that too, on our first visit to the park, but now the traffic jams are just impediments to fishing.

Soda Butte Creek is named for the twenty-feet-high limestone cone formed by one of the park's many geothermal springs. It sits just off the road, and there we passed a Yellowstone Bus going in the opposite direction. After a forty-year absence, these bright yellow vehicles are touring the park again. They were built by the White Motor Company in the late thirties and were gone by the mid sixties. In 2007, the park restored eight of these vehicles and put them back in service. These fourteen-seat touring buses are in high demand with park visitors.

We passed the creek's roadside confluence with the Lamar River. Easy access fills this spot with fishermen, and yet it consistently produces. As we sped by, the Lamar Valley opened to our left. This is one of the best places in the park to view large animals. A three-hundred-strong herd of bison roamed its fertile grassland that day. Pronghorn grazed in small groups nearby. On a past visit, we watched the Druid wolf pack push a nervous elk herd across the valley and into the far timber. On another trip, we observed a grizzly on a kill near the river.

At the end of the valley, the Lamar flows into a short, boulder-filled canyon about a mile above the Lamar River Bridge. Viking dropped Moyski and me off at the first pullout below the bridge, then sped off to catch up with the others. We sat on roadside rocks and donned our waders. Our quarter-mile hike to the river was blocked by a small herd of bison feeding on tall grass along the edge of a wet, desiccating pond. We skirted around the animals and soon were at the river's edge, looking downstream where a canyon wall required us to cross the river and fish from the far bank.

Moyski led. Taller and younger, he had a better chance to pick the way across. Wearing a jaunty hat that arced down in front and back, he moved fluidly into the stream. When he was about six feet ahead, I stepped into the river. I felt the immediate hard push of water against my legs. My waders kept out the wetness but not the cold of the Lamar; my skin transformed to goose bumps and leg muscles tightened. Anchoring my feet between stones, I leaned into the current and tried to keep up with Moyski. The flow loudly burbled off my legs and drowned Moyski's verbal directions. Tentatively, I moved further from the bank and soon was in deeper water.

It is not the depth that makes a crossing difficult, it's the flow. I have been in knee-deep water that swept me off my feet and chest-high water that I easily negotiated. That day, the waist-deep water was challenging but not impossible, and we made the crossing. Neither Moyski nor I use a wading staff. That is one accommodation to age that we are not yet willing to make.

On the far bank, we worked lines through our rod guides and tied on flies. Moyski chose to stay on top with a hopper, and I would work my Little Brown Trout on sinking tip line.

Again, Moyski led, giving me a chance to observe him work the water. Moyski is one of the best fishermen I have ever seen, often rivaling the Fishmaster himself. Soon he was into a good fish. I let my fly hang in the current and watched. With more panache than a red-caped matador, Moyski parried with the fish. When it swam left, Moyski moved his rod tip to the right. When it reversed to the right, Moyski circled his rod up and over to the left. To and fro, fish and rod tip danced over the moving water. He pressured the fish from a low, sidearm angle, only raising the rod tip when it ran, then with full upstretched arm, reached the rod skyward and let the fish have its head. When the fish settled into deep water behind a boulder, Moyski again pressed it from the side, forcing the fish to use its long swim muscles to resist the relentless strain of his deep-bending fly rod.

There is a moment at the end of the fight when both the fish and fisherman know that it's over. The fish can no longer resist the ache in its muscles and surrenders. It was then that Moyski raised his rod tip high and lifted the fish's head out of the water. In one graceful motion, he extended his rod arm back, and as the rod tip arched towards the fish, he dropped to one knee, reached his net forward, and eased the fish into it. The battle won, Moyski looked back at me, smiled, and held the fish high. Then he bent over, extracted the hook, and carefully released a sixteen-inch Yellowstone cutthroat.

We continued working downstream, each taking a fish here and one there, long stretches with nothing, then a run with several. That was typical of the Lamar—fishless stretches and then fish aplenty, unpredictable and changing every day.

Eventually we came to the confluence with Slough Creek. You could hear it before you saw it. The creek's canyon opened from the right with water rushing through large boulders, creating cascades and pockets. Slough Creek extends almost a mile up a quick-rising canyon. We have fished this pocket water several times before, always catching many small fish in the fast water. Any fly will work; it is a tough place for a fish to live, and in the swift current, they don't have time to examine your offering. Ten years ago, I could hop the three- or four-foot distance from rock to rock. I was quite a sport about it. But now, I must climb down one, wade a yard through waist-deep water, and climb up the next. It is a slow, laborious process but still well worth the effort.

Where the fast water of Slough Creek slams into the Lamar, it creates a deep hole. Despite gin-clear water, you cannot see the bottom as it blends into blue, then black. I ran my streamer as deep as I could but still didn't reach the depths. No matter … eager fish shot out of them and hit the Little Brown Trout. Even on top, Moyski's hopper worked, taking fish hidden under ledges and from the shadow water behind boulders.

We worked side by side until I had the urge to move on. While Moyski continued purging the plunge pool of its last trout, I moved up and into the flow of Slough Creek and began to cross. It is all rocks and boulders there, but there are too many gaps to walk across. So, I got into the hard flow of waist-deep water and inched my way along, using rocks as backstops to pin my feet to the bottom. Fifteen minutes later, I was on the other side. There I sat on a smooth boulder to wait for Moyski.

I basked in the warm sun on a skin-temperature day. Sunbeams danced on the Lamar's riffles like sparkling diamonds. Flying insects became whirling points of light, giving dimension to invisible air. A water ouzel picked bugs from the rocky currents, which moments before had been such a challenge for me to cross. I watched it bob and go under, then surface a few feet away with a wiggly in its beak.

The gurgling sound of flowing water made me wonder how long the rocks, canyon, and river had been there. Thoughts of eons … eons of time … of deep time, melted my mind into a still reverie. It was so sublimely pleasant that a thought as subtle as birdsong on the wind came to my mind and I wondered, "Could this be what heaven is like?"

I thought, perhaps heaven doesn't just come at the end of life. Perhaps you've been there and didn't know it. Perhaps you're there right now! I believe there is a being inside us all that waits only for a subtle moment—the smell of a wildflower, the cry of an eagle, the rise of a fish, or a perfect day—to awaken.

I hear others talk of heaven in ambiguous, euphoric ways. Yet, they can never really tell you much about it. For them, it seems to hold all hope for the uncertainties of life, or it is the promise for the end of suffering. A place where, when death takes a loved one, it is comforting to park the dearly departed.

But that is not what heaven is to me. That day on the Lamar and many days that I fish, I am in heaven. I've told my church friends that, but they don't believe me. They say that heaven is greater than anything we can experience on earth. But I wonder: What could be greater than the perfect moment? I am completely absorbed in that moment when I fish. How could anything be greater than that?

"Well, you'll catch more fish," they say. Catching more fish doesn't matter! If I caught a fish on every cast, I would quit fishing. There needs to be incertitude in the pursuit of fish. The writer Ted Leeson said it best, "Fishing is the impassioned anticipation of an uncertain thing." And, more than that for me … it is the wonder of it all … and the greater wonder still, that I am a part of it!

Moyski crossed, smiled, and silently we moved downstream on the Lamar. Immediately below the confluence, we got into more fish. We caught and released eight or so—our best spot yet. Then we worked a long stretch absent of fish, a piscatorial desert. Eventually, the river narrowed to just twenty feet across, as house-sized boulders on our side pinched the opposite canyon wall. A gushing chasm of unfishable water flowed through. This might have been the end of the hike for us and the start of a difficult journey back upstream, but the boulder field on the right bank was negotiable. After scampering about a bit, we came out into Rainbow Alley … and there was Viking!

At least we thought it was Viking. At first we weren't sure because the apparition before us was covered in sun-protecting gloves, Buff face mask, dark sunglasses, and a big, droopy hat. Ah, the Norsemen, how they have to protect their delicate skin!

Viking was into a good fish, and after he released it, he greeted us and removed all doubt. Like Stanley finding Livingstone, we had contacted the Venerable Fly Tyers of Rainbow Alley, a breed like no other.

As we fished and mingled with our club members for the remainder of the day, we learned that they, too, had caught many fish. The "Alley Boys" discovered fish bellies filled with ants, although none of the Boys had seen any in the air or on the water. One by one they switched to ant patterns and "slayed" the trout … rainbow, cutthroat, cutbow … it didn't matter.

As long shadows fell on the Lamar, we hiked the uphill mile to our vehicles. We drove along the Northeast Entrance Road in darkness, the traffic gone, but the drive lengthened by the ubiquitous, road-crossing bison.

That night over dinner at the Beartooth Café, six good friends recounted stories of the day's fishing. The discovery of the ants was told, complete with hand gestures of pumping fish stomachs. The fish of the day turned out to be Doc Scott's eighteen-inch rainbow. Doc's quiet voice had us leaning in to hear the tale of how he caught it. Then Moyski and I held court with our stories of river crossings, rock climbing, and trout shooting up from the depths.

The Beartooth prides itself with a hundred varieties of craft beer. That night the *Vulnerable* Fly Tyers eagerly sampled many! As the brew flowed, the stories got louder, gestures wilder, and eventually we were asked to leave.

Taking our act outside, we began the short walk back to the Antlers. In the darkness and between the laughter, Bald Eagle said, "Look how bright the stars are!"

"Yes," I added, "and there is a meteor shower tonight, the Perseids. The son of Zeus will be throwing rocks at the earth."

We found a soft, grassy spot, and lay on our backs. Our minds reeled as we watched the night sky and took turns pointing out each falling star.

Viking produced a bottle of whiskey, took a swig, and passed it around. The aurora borealis appeared low in the northern sky. It climbed higher until a rippling neon veil glowed overhead. Amazed, Tobias asked, "Is this real or is it the whiskey?"

"What kind of whiskey was that?" Hellman queried.

Viking gave a knowing laugh while Doc Scott retrieved the empty bottle and read the label. "You aren't going to believe this. It says, 'Northern Lights Whiskey.'"

There was a long silence … before Moyski asked, "Does anyone have a bottle of Naked Lady Whiskey?"

# WHY I FISH

I am often asked why I fish. Two kinds of people ask this question. The first kind just don't see the attraction. They are drawn to other pursuits like coupon collecting or golf, and they just don't have that inner, inexplicable call to fish. The other kind have some moral objection to fishing. They buy their food at supermarkets, on little foam trays wrapped in cellophane, checking to see if it is wild or farm-raised. It is easy to forget that life feeds on life when someone else does the killing for you.

Or they may be vegans, in which case I must concede the moral high ground! I have no argument, other than to admit that I am not as evolved as they are.

Once, my friend Hellman was fishing with his young daughter. After catching and releasing a fish, she asked, "Daddy, do fish scream?"

He said, "No honey, because if they did, we wouldn't be doing this!" There are studies that suggest that fish don't feel pain or fright. Yet, I doubt these. I have no illusion that the pleasure I gain from fishing comes at a cost to the fish. I try to mitigate that with catch and release and barbless hooks, but I know it's at the fish's expense. I will just have to carry that burden.

I fish because I am fascinated by fish and the world in which they live. I have always been this way; my oldest memories are from the water's edge. I want to connect to the world of fish, to briefly dance with them, to hold them in my hand, and marvel at their beauty—then carefully release them back into their resplendent underwater world. I want to join them there and feel the cool, luxurious flow of liquid along my body and detect the tiniest changes in pressure. I want to see light filtered through a column of water. To have my food presented along the conveyor belt of moving water … to choose or to reject. To see the seasons come and go. To watch plants dance in the current and pick tiny bits of food from their leaves. I want to feel what it is like to scrape my belly along smooth, bright pebbles and find the tiniest of insects crawling about. I want to blow bubbles and leave rings. I fish because … I can't turn myself into a trout!

# GENESIS

"My mentor was a genius," said John Long, our instructor, about Bill Waara, the man who taught him to make bamboo fly rods.

"I wish my mentor was a genius," I muttered, after watching Bald Eagle try to put a screwdriver through his hand. I tried to offer advice but got a scowl in return. So, I walked over to the coffeepot and refilled both our cups. I turned and paused, taking in the whole room and all its activity. I thought of the day, two months earlier, when the seed was planted.

"Attendance at the Genesis School of Rod Making is mandatory," Bald Eagle had said. Yes, it was all his idea. He wanted to make a bamboo fly rod and had for years searched the country for a school and schedule that fit us. When he heard of the Genesis program, right here in our home state of Michigan, he eagerly phoned me. "We have to do this; we have to learn to make a bamboo fly rod!"

"Why do we have to do this?" I asked.

"Because it will be the culmination of your education as a fly-fisher-man, Archer," said Bald Eagle, the man who has taught me everything. "You know how to fish, you know all the river things: trout, forage, flow, and all. You know your bugs—you even know their Latin names. You tie all of your own flies and make leaders, too!"

"So now you want me to whittle a fly rod out of some old, gnarly stick of bamboo?" I asked.

"You don't whittle it. You plane it, six triangular strips, tapered and glued together."

"How long does this rod whittling class take?"

"Six days, six full days … for you, maybe longer," he said.

So, I agreed, not because I wanted to make a bamboo fly rod, not because I wanted to finish my education, but because I wanted to do something with my friend for a whole week.

Eventually mid-April came, and after a long, cold Michigan winter, the class date finally arrived. I rose early, dressed, and with a cup of coffee, waited in my easy chair for Bald Eagle. He was early—a full thirty minutes early. Excitedly he helped me load my stuff into his SUV, and before I had even closed the car door, we were rolling. He backed out of my drive, turned north, and headed for NettieBay Lodge.

Five hours later, we turned off County Road 638, west of the small village of Hawks, onto a gravel road that took us to a classic northern-Michigan lake resort. Complete with lodge, cabins, and beach, it was nicely tucked into a small bay on Nettie Lake. The hundred-acre lake was lined with cedars and tall white pines. Clapboard cottages sat close to the water's edge, just off a fine sand beach. The lake was still frozen and snow covered. On the shore lay the docks and boats that would be returned to the water in early June.

As Rod parked along the gravel drive, two men appeared out of nowhere and eagerly greeted us. They introduced themselves as our instructors, John Long and Ron Barch. John was about six feet tall, two hundred pounds, with a full head of brown hair and smooth skin that made him look ten years younger than his sixty years. I offered my hand; he shook it and grinned. Ron was in his early fifties, balding, short, and thin—a wired bundle of energy. He wore an easy smile and talked in a quick but friendly manner. I would later learn that he was the editor of the *Planing Form*, the newsletter for the bamboo rod making craft. In their professional lives, John was an electrician for Detroit Edison and Ron a high school teacher for alternative students—making him well prepared to teach the likes of us!

The school was set in the walk-out level of NettieBay Lodge, a fieldstone and log home, owned by Mark and Jackie Schuler. While Mark participated in the class, Jackie provided hearty, home-cooked meals. We ate family style in a large dining room adjacent to our workspace.

In the course of the week, we learned that the lodge hosted many training programs, called "learning vacations." These were as diverse as birding, photography, and stone masonry. The lodge itself was built by students of the log-home-building school. The Schulers had it down—they were able to extend their short summer resort season into a year-round source of revenue. They even had the laborers who built their home pay them for the privilege of doing it!

We were housed in one of the lodge's lakeside cabins. Free until dinner, we met the other students as they arrived and settled in. There were six others, all good guys, all eager to learn. After one of Jackie's delicious meals, we spent the evening getting acquainted. The conversations were ones of guarded excitement. Everyone was glad to be there and eager for the program to begin. Yet, there was a bit of uncertainty, as each harbored the doubt, "Will I be up to the task of making a bamboo fly rod?" Tomorrow would give us the answer.

Day One. Morning came and the program began. After a wholesome breakfast, we adjourned to the classroom where four workbenches had been set up, two students to each. On the benches were a variety of tools: screwdrivers, knives, rubber hammers, vises, hand planes, and a planing form.

Rod and I quickly grabbed a bench together. Ron and John handed each bench team a stick of bamboo that measured twelve feet long by three inches in diameter. We learned that the stick is called a culm and is a special species of bamboo called Tonkin cane. Its Latin name is *Arundinaria amabilis*, which translates to the "lovely reed." It is imported from a sixty-square-mile area in China, near the Gulf of Tonkin—yes, that Gulf of Tonkin! Of the fifteen hundred species of bamboo worldwide, it is the most suitable to make fine split-cane bamboo fly rods.

Ron and John told us that bamboo is a fast-growing grass, yet it is harder than most hardwoods. Long, continuous fibers run the length of the stalk, like a stick of celery, only packed much tighter. They are held together by a matrix of a natural, plastic-like substance called lignin. Every twelve to eighteen inches, the fibers are interrupted by a cross-sectional dam called a node.

Our first task was to split the culm lengthwise with a dullish, thick knife. Then Rod took one half and I the other. Next, we took the pieces outside and scorched the outer enamel-like skin with a propane torch. This drove out moisture and colored the bamboo a rich caramel. Back inside, we cut our halves into two equal lengths and then further split them. We drove a sharpened screwdriver into the cane at intervals, twisting and forcing the strips apart. The goal was to get twelve one-quarter-inch-wide strips—six strips for the tip section and six for the butt section of a two-piece fly rod.

We adjourned for lunch. Around the big table in the dining room, and amidst another robust meal, we had much to talk about. We had begun work, and so far the tasks were pleasant and manageable. Ron told us that there were more than a thousand steps in the process of making a split-cane bamboo fly rod. And, if we did each step well, in just a week's time, we would be able to hold in our hands a highly functioning and beautiful fly rod.

Excitedly we returned to our benches and aligned the strips in front of us. John told us that the nodes would cause problems from the beginning to the end of the rod-making process. He instructed us to line up six strips and slide every other one, so that no two nodes were next to each other, in a three-by-three configuration. He then had us cut the strips to length for half of a seven-foot-six-inch rod. This would be the tip section; we redid this process with six more strips for the butt section.

Next, we filed each node flat with a sharp wood file, then turned it over and recessed the back with a round file. We set up heat guns and John showed us how to heat-treat each node. He demonstrated the point where the lignin in the cane breaks down enough to compress the nodes. While still hot, the node was placed in a vise and pressed flat. Then he rotated the strip ninety degrees and pressed out any lateral bends.

It looked easy—it was not! We each found that there was a fine point between getting the bamboo plastic or burning the crap out of it. Also, you needed bare fingers to feel the heat in the cane and the exact moment when it surrenders its stiffness … bare fingers that are handling sharp edges near a very hot flame. Frequent trips to the first aid station were the order of the day. Yet we soldiered on, bandaged fingers and all. By the end of the day, we had each flattened and straightened all thirty-six nodes on our twelve strips.

After work we went outdoors. John and Ron had a dozen bamboo fly rods for us to cast. We spaced out over a snowy lawn and began casting. I had never cast a bamboo rod; in fact, I had never even held one. While the others oohed and aahed at the rods, I found their action to be slow and languorous and began to wonder why I signed up for a class to make them. At that time, my everyday rod was a Sage RPL Plus, a very stiff graphite rod that was the polar opposite of bamboo. My casting stroke did not agree with this new material. In addition, I was a poor caster, and the graphite's fast action hid my sins well. But bamboo did not; my attempts at casting resulted in S curves of line overhead until they fell in knotted piles at my feet.

That evening, we set the routine that would carry through the week. After a delicious family-style dinner, we adjourned to a large sitting room. Over beer and drinks, we discussed the day's events, talked about fly rods and fly fishing, world events, and women. All too soon, heads were nodding, and eight tired men dragged their weary bodies off to bed.

Day Two. We took our quarter-inch strips and hand planed the sides and bottoms, removing bends and getting a uniform square dimension. Now we had to turn the squares into triangles. Ron had a machine, a beveler, comprised of a horizontal infeed/outfeed table, a router motor, and a blade that cut a perfect sixty-degree angle. After several passes through the beveler, each strip had a level-equilateral-triangular cross section.

Our instructors had us take our strips and wrap them in a Rube Goldberg device designed by famous rod maker Everett Garrison. This device was called a binder and had a heavy thread drive belt. As you turned a crank, the belt spun the six strips while spiraling light cotton thread around them, binding them together. Next, the bound strips went into an oven. Not a kitchen oven, but a long, narrow, homemade, sheet metal oven that could accommodate the bound fifty-inch strips. A heat gun we inserted into a hole in the top baked the strips at three hundred and fifty degrees for fifteen minutes. Before the time expired, you could smell the pleasant, sweet odor of burning sugars as the heat drove moisture out of the cane and facilitated a chemical change in the lignin. The end result was that the cane strips were lighter, stiffer, and straighter. When cooled, we removed the thread and were ready for final planing.

The end of the day again found us outdoors, casting bamboo rods. I still didn't like them and was perplexed when Ron pressed each of us to choose the taper that we would like to make. All rods would be seven-foot-six-inch five-weights, but there were many choices of tapers that fit that criterion. In short, a taper defined the cross-sectional dimensions that gave the finished rod a line weight and specific action—an action of "slow, slower, or slowest" as far as I was concerned. Bald Eagle chose Lyle Dickerson's 7615 taper. The other students all found something they liked—but not me. Again, I questioned why I was doing this. Ron Barch, sensing my discomfort, suggested that I make the Paul Young Perfectionist taper. I acquiesced, on the weak theory that since there wasn't one there to try, I might actually like it.

Day Three. We set up our planing forms. A planing form consists of two sixty-inch long, one-inch square lengths of cold rolled steel. They sit side by side and are attached together with a pin and two setscrews at five-inch increments. A sixty-degree tapered v-groove runs down the length of it. The setscrews (one pusher and one puller) are used to set the depth of that v-groove at each station along the length of the planing form. This will determine the tapered cross section of the rod. The taper itself is a formula proscribed by the original rod maker and is expressed in thousands of an inch at each of the five-inch stations.

The planing forms were set and then checked by our instructors. Then we each took one of our strips, put it into the v-groove, and ran a razor-sharp hand plane down its length, removing a thin curl of bamboo. As we planed, we turned the strips from side to side, with the outer edge of the strip always in one side of the groove and never planed. We removed bamboo until it was flush with the top of the form. The strip then conformed perfectly to the set taper, or so we hoped. Each strip took us about an hour. It was a slow process for the inexperienced, with frequent checks on our progress to ensure that the proper angles were maintained. The plane blades had to be frequently sharpened by hand, also taking time. Of course, there were cuts, accidents, and more trips to the first aid station.

Day Four. We continued planing, pressured by knowing that we had to glue up at the end of the day. Late in the day, as each student finished, Ron or John would check their work, then lay out the strips, lightly sand the interior apex, and then lavishly apply a mixture of Resorcinol glue. The strips were rolled together, taped at both ends, and again placed in the Garrison binder. We turned the crank, applying binding thread in one continuous spiral wrap, then put the bound strips back in the binder and counter wrapped another spiral of thread. Each section was then carefully tied off and hung from a hook to dry. By the end of the day, eight students stood admiring sixteen bound and glued sections of potential cane rods. Too tired to cast, we dined, drank beer and spirits, and went to bed early.

Day Five. An hour early, we were in the shop excitedly waving about our new hardened bamboo rod sections. After breakfast, we removed the thread, scraped off the glue that adhered to the outside, and for the first time got a feel for what these rods would become.

We carefully cut our sections to length, then took each to Ron who placed it in a small machinist lathe and removed cane for the nickel-silver ferrules that would slide on each end and hold the two sections together. Then the ferrules were glued with epoxy, slid onto the rod, and their slit tabs secured with binding thread.

Next came the cork grips. We reamed half-inch cork rings and slid them into position near the butt of the rod. We applied epoxy and pressed the rings tightly together with a special cork press. An hour later, the glue was dry. We placed the butt section in the lathe and removed cork with sandpaper to shape the grip to our individual taste. Reel seats were next. Ron had a varied selection of wood inserts and we chose grain patterns and colors to enhance the beauty of our nearly finished rods. We glued them in place along with nickel-silver bands and butt caps.

Later that afternoon, when all the glue was dry, our fly rods were complete except for wrapped guides and varnish. We fine-tuned the fit of the ferrules and assembled the sections. As we waved them about, we got a good feel for how our rods would cast.

Day Six. Ideally at this point, we would've attached guides with thread wraps along the length of the rod. But in a week-long school this was not possible, so we would do this later at home. A shortcut for varnishing had to be accommodated as well. Traditionally bamboo fly rods are finished by dipping each section into a tube of varnish and then slowly extracting it so that a thin, blemish-free coat adheres to the surface. Since that takes several coats and days to dry, we used a simpler technique. We applied multiple coats of fast-drying, wipe-on, tung oil varnish, which we rubbed until it warmed enough to penetrate into the bamboo.

While wiping another coat onto my rod, I asked Bald Eagle, "What will you name your rod when you are done?"

"I don't know," he said. "You?"

"I will call it the 'Genesis' after the name of the school where I built it."

"I wish I had thought of that!" he exclaimed.

I then suggested to Bald Eagle, who at the time suffered from bouts of A-Fib, that he name his rods after heart conditions, and I laid out the scheme. "'A-Fib'" would be a good middle-of-the-road fly rod, such as the seven-foot-six-inch five-weight that you just made. 'A-Flutter' could be for one with a bit of a whippier action. Then there is 'Murmur' for that six-foot three-weight. And the top of the line, that eight-foot seven-weight steelhead rod, 'Coronary Thrombosis!'"

He didn't like my idea and said, "If I fished a rod like that, I just might have one!" I guessed he didn't want to hear about the "Open Heart Surgery" or "Quadruple Bypass" models! Instead, he decided to label his rods by the name of the original maker and taper. So, there was his "Dickerson 7615," and later the "Young Midge" and "Payne 98."

Finally, Saturday morning came. We shared our last breakfast. It was time to leave, but no one was in a hurry to go. The week together, performing a common task, had drawn us all close. We all had finished our rods, dispelling our early doubts. As we lined up and jostled to take a group photo, I felt a special bond with these good men. I had come to this school a bit reluctantly. Despite myself, I thoroughly enjoyed the week. The process of making bamboo fly rods suited me, and I eagerly looked forward to casting mine. We lingered, admired each other's handiwork, and exchanged contact information. Then slowly, one by one, we left.

# WHY BAMBOO

In 2000, I attended the Genesis School of Rod Making, conducted by John Long and Ron Barch. Under their instruction, I built my first split-cane bamboo fly rod. I knew nothing about bamboo rods before taking that weeklong class, but I have fished with little else since. I simply love making and fishing bamboo fly rods. In this essay, I give my reasons why I think they fish better than anything else.

The history of fly rod making goes back several centuries and is best recorded in England, with the writings of Berners, Cotton, and Walton. The earliest rods were simple cuttings from streamside branches—willow, ash, and alder served well. The line was twisted horsehair and no longer than the length of the branch. Good branches were saved, taken home, and worked with a knife to remove bark and lumps.

Eventually crafted wood replaced branches. Greenheart and lance-wood were two of the most popular. They were relatively light, flexible, and strong. They were shaved to control the progression from the light, narrow tip to the thicker, heavier butt—the first attempt at a taper. In fifteenth-century England, rods approximately fourteen feet long, matched with an equal length of line, were used. The fly was simply swung out or, if the rod was limber enough, flicked back overhead once, then out onto the water.

In the 1700s, wire loops were attached to rods to control the line. Joints, the first attempts at ferrules, were added for transportability. Silk replaced horsehair as line. Rudimentary winches, or reels, allowed for more line and greater casting distances.

Rod material changed in the 1800s, from the native woods to lighter and more elastic species imported from the Empire. Bamboo, in the form of Calcutta cane from the India trade, was introduced. It was not split and glued as we know it today but like the cane poles of our youth.

Eventually they were split and glued. Samuel Phillippe of Easton, Pennsylvania, is credited with the first such multisided rod. In 1874, gunsmith Hiram Leonard, of Bangor, Maine, perfected the six-strip, hexagonal rod. This soon became the standard in split-cane rod making and remains so today.

The next improvement was a new species of bamboo. Tonkin cane was first imported in 1895. Within twenty years, it replaced Calcutta cane in rod making. Of the more than one thousand species of bamboo in the world, Tonkin cane, *Arundinaria amabilis* (the lovely reed), because of its dense power fibers and great spacing between nodes, proved to be the most suitable for fly rod making.

Bamboo is a remarkable material. It is essentially a fast-growing grass. It has long, longitudinal fibers encased in a natural resin called lignin. It is harder than most hardwoods, unbelievably strong, can flex deeply without breaking, and quickly rebound. At just four years of age, it is forty feet tall, three inches in diameter, and ready for harvest. It is cut by hand, sorted, bundled, and shipped to America and Europe, where rod makers eagerly await its arrival.

Most early bamboo rods were made to facilitate the popular style of fishing at the time: downstream wet fly fishing. Three-sectioned, six- or seven-weight rods, nine feet or longer in length were able to cast a trace of several wet flies downstream and swing them across the current. The fisherman then took a couple of steps downstream, backcast, and did it again. These rods were long, heavy, and very flexible. They are still around. You can buy them at garage sales or perhaps find them in the back of grandpa's tackle closet.

As fishing styles changed, dry fly fishing became more popular. Innovative rod makers like Everett Garrison, Lyle Dickerson, and Paul Young began making shorter rods with crisper actions to deliver small dry flies to rising fish. This golden age of bamboo fly rods began in the 1930s and continued through World War II. After the war, returning GIs took to recreation—and fishing in particular—with zeal. Bamboo rod makers couldn't keep up with the demand. Because of the Chinese Civil War and subsequent American embargo, Tonkin cane was nearly impossible to obtain and prewar supplies quickly dwindled.

Rod makers looked for another source of material. Steel was tried and proved unsatisfactory—imagine that! Then, two aerospace engineers, Glen Havens and Arthur Howald, independently introduced fiberglass. Almost overnight, it took over the rod market. It flexed much like bamboo and was easy to mass-produce. Yet, bamboo remained the standard as fiberglass rods were made to imitate its action.

In 1973, the Fenwick Company introduced graphite fly rods, and other manufacturers quickly followed suit. Again, the early graphite rods were made to imitate bamboo. But soon this much lighter and stiffer material began dancing to its own beat. Graphite, when flexed, returns to its neutral state much quicker than either bamboo or fiberglass. Rods were made longer, lighter, and stiffer. The ideal of faster, stiffer action rods became a near obsession. These rods bent near the tip only, and the great line speed produced by short, quick strokes allowed even poor casters to make distant casts.

So why bamboo, today? What advantages does it have over modern synthetic materials? As we have seen, graphite rods have gotten progressively lighter and stiffer. Compared to graphite, bamboo is heavy and flexible. And that is precisely the advantage that it has!

Look at it this way: If I challenged you to a stone-throwing contest, what size stone would you choose? The smallest, lightest pebble you could find, or a stone with the right "heft"? One that feels good in your hand, one heavy enough to cut through the air, yet light enough that you could still achieve maximum arm speed? In mathematical terms, the equation for this is $E_k = \frac{1}{2}mv^2$—kinetic energy equals one half mass times velocity squared. The greater the energy, the farther the stone goes! You certainly don't want to lose the arm speed, but you do want the mass.

Bamboo has that mass. In trout rods of four-, five-, and six-weight, from six to eight feet in length, it can't be beaten for either castability or all-around fishing. In this range, a four-ounce bamboo rod can be comfortably fished all day long, so what is the advantage of a one-and-a-half-ouncer? None!

A fly rod combines two simple tools: a lever and a spring. It is a lever because it is longer than your arm and a spring because it loads, bends, and releases, propelling fly line forward. Graphite rods, because material lightness allows them to be long, favor the lever. More flexible bamboo rods, while heavier, favor the spring.

So how is this an advantage? Number one: casting range. The heavier self-weight of bamboo requires no line loading to cast in close. The rod loads itself, allowing you to make short casts of even just the tippet. For longer casts, the bamboo spring flexes deeply, often all the way into the grip. It is a deep, slow stroke, but allows you to cast long distances.

Number two: roll casting. Again, the self-weight of bamboo helps to load the rod even when static line does not.

Number three: accuracy. A seven-foot-six-inch bamboo rod is roughly equivalent to a nine-foot graphite rod in terms of casting ability (spring versus lever); errant hand movements are not accentuated by the longer lever distance, thus making the shorter rod more accurate.

Number four: presentation. The long, slow stroke of a bamboo cast and its lower line speed allow for a much more delicate presentation, allowing the fly to float down and gently land on the water. You're not banging it out there, you are laying it out there!

Number five: tippet protection. The more flexible bamboo acts as a shock absorber for a hard take, allowing you to fish finer tippets and smaller flies. This is also a benefit while fighting fish. More pressure can be applied with the confidence that the rod will absorb surges and runs.

Those are the practical benefits. Now what about the esoteric ones, like beauty? Who considers plastic beautiful? Nobody! Bamboo is beautiful. Whether flamed or blonde, it has the beauty and grace of finely finished wood under warm, amber coats of varnish, which, by the way, smell good, too. Subtle-colored guide wraps, nickel-silver hardware, and reel seats of butternut, walnut, maple, or plum coordinate and enhance the overall elegance of a split-cane rod.

Finally, there is tradition—one hundred and fifty years' worth. When you hold a fine bamboo fly rod, you connect to generations of fishermen and rod makers. People who valued, preserved, and treasured the care and crafts-manship that produced such an elegant tool. Although designed to catch fish, a bamboo fly rod catches the eye and imagination of all who appreciate beauty fused with function.

# STEFAN SHOT LAST

My favorite picture of myself is one of me holding a brook trout. Not that the fish was a trophy, it was only four inches long, but the photo captured a smile on my face that reflected the joy of doing what I love most: fly fishing on a warm, summer day. It is also special because it was taken by my nephew, Stefan. At the time, he was twelve years old and we were on a fishing trip together. His mother, Julie, had asked me to take him for a week and teach him how to fly-fish. His father, my brother, Mike, worked hard and long as a contractor in our hometown of Green Lake, Wisconsin. Mike was busy during the summer building season, and while he loved to duck hunt, fishing was not as high on his list of favorite activities.

But fishing was at the top of Stefan's list. You are either born with the fishing bug or you are not. I had watched Stefan since he was a tot sneak along the water's edge with a stick, poking at small fish and frogs hiding in the rocks and weeds there. He turned stones over and crayfish darted out. Trying to hand catch them, he often toppled in and had to be retrieved by the belt of his pants. It never deterred him; he'd be right back at it as soon as you turned your back. I knew what drove him; I had that drive as a child myself.

At twelve, Stefan was ready to learn to fly-fish. I picked him up at the airport and drove him to my home in suburban Detroit. We spent the next couple of days with the precursors: casting lessons in the backyard, fishing poppers and ant patterns to bluegill in the pond, and learning fly-tying in the evening.

Finally, we were ready for our trip north. We packed the Fishwagon with enough gear, clothing, and food for a four-day excursion. As we pulled out of the drive, we gave each other a big high five and then smiled for the next three hours, all the way to Grayling. There we stopped at the Fly Factory, the fly shop housed in an old log building on the bank of the Au Sable River. Some form of this establishment had been on this spot since the 1930s, when Sailor Bill Huddleston sold his hand-tied flies from an old, parked school bus. Before that, Chippewa Indian Chief David Shoppenagon camped at this site and sold fine canoe paddles that he carved from maple planks.

The Fly Factory was packed from floor to ceiling with rods, reels, and nets. Full muskrat and beaver pelts hung in cabinets and other furs and feathers filled their drawers. A display case with two hundred bins held flies of every size, shape, and color imaginable. Taxidermic fish and animals adorned the walls. Stefan wandered the shop with glazed eyes and mouth held open. He had found the Holy Grail of his piscatorial pursuit. He could have lingered all day, but I moved him along. We purchased a few necessities and a couple of whimsies for Stefan and then were on our way.

We headed west of town on Highway M-72 to the Manistee River, crossed the bridge, and turned in to the campground there. I chose to take the new fly-fisherman to this spot because it was wide and shallow and there were plenty of gullible, small fish. Stefan could easily wade and cast with room all around.

After setting up camp, we grabbed our rods and reels and hurried down to the stream. We wet-waded in the warm August afternoon, working our way upstream for about a half mile before turning back down. It was too hot really and fishing was slow until the last hour. We were almost back to the campsite when a few tiny, blue-winged olives started to emerge, and small fish eagerly took them with splashy rises. Stefan fooled several little brook trout with a #20 Griffith Gnat, his first trout caught on a fly.

It was dark by the time we climbed out of the stream. Stefan built a fire and I cooked a quick dinner of bacon and eggs. We fell asleep to the sounds of flowing water and whip-poor-wills in the white pines that surrounded us.

We were up before breakfast, wading downstream in hopes of a trico spinner fall. Above the bridge, we found tricos and tiny blue-winged olives on the water. Small fish eagerly fed on them, and again the Griffith Gnat worked its magic. We continued downstream, hoping for bigger fish. Two bends below, we found fish rising and fooled them with deer hair caddis. Our big fish of the morning was an eight-inch brown trout.

At noon, we were back at the camp, cooking brats on the grill. After our meal, I ceremoniously presented Stefan with the official Fishwagon hat, a ball cap with the crest embroidered with an image of the Fishwagon and words "Fishwagon Fly Fishing."

That afternoon, the water was above seventy degrees and too warm to fish. At the campsite picnic table, we continued the tying lessons that had become a daily event during Stefan's visit. After a couple of hours, we broke camp and headed for the North Branch of the Au Sable, hoping to find cooler water. Heading east on M-72, we saw a road sign saying, "PRISON AREA DO NOT PICK UP HITCHHIKERS." I pulled over and directed Stefan to stand in front of the sign with his thumb out, took the picture, and made a mental note to send it to his mother—just to show that her son was in good hands with his Uncle Dave.

We pulled into the Jackson Hole campsite on the North Branch. Clad in our sandals and shorts, we hiked a mile upstream along the fisherman's trail. We fished for about an hour, but the water was too warm and no fish showed. Low, threatening, dark clouds rolled in from the west; the wind gusted and a heavy rain began to fall. When lightning struck, we moved off the water and to the shelter of tall, streamside hemlocks. We were under cover just in time. As the storm raged, thunder and lightning were nearly simultaneous, and we could smell cordite in the air. It was as dark as any night. I tried to hold him back, but Stefan bolted for the truck. I watched him run through the woods, lit frequently by bursts of lightning that gave the effect of strobe-light dancing—he was here, then he was there, then way over there, and soon he was out of sight. I didn't follow; the woods were thick and my legs not as nimble as his. I couldn't have caught him anyway.

Finally, the worst of the storm passed. As the rain abated, I hiked back to camp. Stefan was there in the Fishwagon, quietly changing out of his wet clothes with a big grin on his face.

Although we had planned to stay the night, I was concerned about driving out in the morrow if more rain fell. There were clay roads and a steep hill to negotiate. We stowed our gear, carefully drove out of the campground and back to the main road, and then returned to the Manistee, hoping to be on the lee side of the storm. This time we pulled into the Goose Creek Trail Camp and drove on to the campsites along the river. At the first site, we found a large, downed tree. It was a fresh fall and undoubtedly happened in the past couple of hours as the storm passed through.

I backed the Fishwagon as tight to the deadfall as I could—even had a couple of branches hanging precariously over it. I then had Stefan wedge himself under the downed tree with just his legs sticking out and snapped another picture for his mother—I'm sure she will appreciate the photo log of his trip.

We moved to the next campsite and set up there. By the time we were ready to fish, the clouds had passed and it was sunny again. We worked the water downstream and soon found several rising fish, obviously invigorated by the rain and cooler water. Together we took ten fish, both brook and brown trout. My best fish came on a deer hair caddis drifted tightly along a downed log. The fish, not large but an insolent fighter, had risen twice before my second drift took it. In the waning light, we hooked several more before darkness drove us off the river. It had been an eventful day and we were soon fast asleep in the cooler night air.

We were out again early the next morning. The river, although a bit turbid, was cooler and the fish more active. They were rising in all the likely spots—along logs and in the bubble lines below sweepers. Stefan was eager and charged from one rising fish to another, putting them down before he could even make a cast.

It was time for another Uncle Dave lesson. "Stefan, if you were fishing for squirrels …"

"Can you fish for squirrels?" he asked.

"No … but if you were, would you just charge over and throw a nut on a string to them?"

"No, that'd scare 'em away," he said.

"That's right, and fish are animals, too. Just because you can't see or hear them, doesn't mean they can't see or hear you. Start approaching a fish like you would a squirrel in a park," I said.

"Let me demonstrate. See that fish rising fifty yards below, along the current seam where the fast water passes the slow, shallow water along the bank? Now follow behind me." Then I slowly and carefully moved downstream to a position about fifty feet above the rising fish. I cast carefully without splashing and picked up quietly. I moved a few feet closer and did it again. With each cast, I moved a bit closer and extended the drift longer until my drift floated over the fish's lie. The fish rose and confidently took my fly. After a brief fight, I brought it to hand, my best of the day, a ten-inch, bright-yellow brown trout.

I don't know who was more impressed with the demonstration, Stefan or me, but he got the message. Then I sat on a log, lit a pipe, and watched him carefully and stealthily work the rising fish around us. He took a half dozen before the morning's action stopped.

About then a canoe rounded the bend with two winsome, bikini-clad, college-aged girls paddling idly. I asked them to stop and explained that I would like to get of picture of them hanging on my nephew's biceps. They laughed, splashed water at me, and paddled on. Too bad … what an addition that would have been to Stefan's photo log—another one I'm sure his mother would have appreciated!

After lunch, we packed up and headed back downstate. During the drive, we relived our adventure together. I reinforced the lessons that I hoped he learned, complimented him on his progress, and expressed gratitude on how well he pitched in and helped around the campsite. Then we promised each other to do this trip again. But, it would never happen. There is just a brief window in a young boy's life, from when he is old enough to when he is encumbered by summer jobs, girls, and August football practices. Nevertheless, on this trip, I had witnessed the budding of a true outdoors sportsman.

But that was not my first experience with my nephew, Stefan, as an outdoorsman. That had happened several years before when Stefan was just three years old. My brother, Mike, and I had been hunting ducks along the

Grand River, south of Lake Puckaway, near our hometown of Green Lake, Wisconsin. We had a good early morning hunt, taking several ducks apiece until the sun burned through a low cloud layer. The resulting blue skies had settled the ducks on the marsh and nearby cornfields; they wouldn't move again until twilight.

So, we packed it in and drove to Mom's house, where I was staying. She prepared and served coffee and breakfast. Over pancakes, we talked of our morning hunt. Soon Stefan wandered in from his house just up the hill. He was excited to hear the tales of our duck hunt and then asked if he could see the ducks we shot. Mike told him that they were in the back of the pickup and that he could go down and see them while we finished breakfast. So off he scampered.

A few minutes later we followed, planning to clean the ducks, our guns, and stow the gear. As we rounded the back of the pickup, we heard a frenzied scuffling inside under the cap. We looked in, and there was Stefan holding a very-much-alive mallard drake by the front of his wings and banging his head on the gunnels of the canoe. Stefan looked up at us and said, "This one's still alive; don't worry, I kill it!"

Then and there we knew he had the hunting instinct—even it was a bit on the raw side for one so young. Apparently the duck had been merely stunned by a single BB to the head and came around an hour later in the back of the pickup, about the time Stefan found it.

Over the ensuing years, as often as I could, I returned to Wisconsin in the fall to hunt with Mike. We always took Stefan with us. Even at a young age, he could rise early, sit in a cold blind all morning, and just generally stay out of trouble. He kept the dog company, counted shells in their boxes, and was often the first to see incoming ducks. In short, he never ruined a hunt and was just fun to have around.

When Stefan turned ten, Mike let him bring along an old family shotgun. My brother had trained him in gun safety and Stefan was very careful with his weapon. Because he was young and a new shooter, we always let him shoot first. So, when incoming ducks came, we waited until Mike said, "Now!" Then Stefan stood up, took aim, and shot. When he finished, we took our shots. It didn't take too many outings before Stefan actually started to hit a few ducks. Yet, we continued that first-shot tradition through his teenage years.

The July that Stefan was seventeen years old, he asked Mike if he could borrow the pickup and drive to Madison to watch the annual Wisconsin Trap Shoot. He was given permission and a few dollars, and off he went. Two days later, an excited Stefan called his dad; he had done more than watch the shoot, he had entered … and he won in his category.

Later that fall, when the opening of duck season came, Stefan, Mike, and I hunted the head-of-the-lake blind together. This blind has been hunted by generations of Jankowskis and Nortons for more than one hundred years. It was built on a point of land purchased by John W. Norton, of the First Wisconsin Cavalry, with his share of the reward from his part in the capture of Jefferson Davis after the Civil War.

We set a new tradition that day. We changed the order of shooting … Stefan, the Wisconsin State Trap Champion, shot last!

# SAVING WHISTLE PIG

"Help me!" yelled Whistle Pig. I looked in the direction of his frantic call and saw nothing. I had seen him there just moments before, when he had been about to step off the end of the island into the Platte River. I rushed over and found him, head below the crest of the island and up to the top of his chest waders in water.

"Pull me out!" he pleaded with more than a little panic in his voice. I sat down on the edge of the island behind him and reached under his arms. I tried to lift, but it was no good. He is a big man, bigger than me, and was mired up to his waist in quicksand—not really quicksand, but the soft muck that collects in the calm water adjacent to the current, like that at the lee of an island.

I saw this once before. I watched my wife and two daughters pulling their kayaks through a shallow slip out of the main current. Where the slip emptied into Boardman Lake, Mary took a step into that same soft sort of detritus and dropped vertically like a rock. Our daughters each managed to grab an arm but not before Mary was up to her neck in water. With difficulty, they pulled her up and out. She was covered in muck up to her chin.

I wondered what would have happened if she had been alone. I think that she would have drowned, unable to swim in that soft, enveloping muck.

It was the same with Whistle Pig now. He didn't seem to be sinking any lower but was unable to get himself out. Unless someone found him, he would tire, drown, starve, or die of old age. Since you don't hear of many missing or disappearing fishermen, this must not be a big problem. But it was a problem for Whistle Pig that day.

I found some footing well wide of his spot and lifted with all my might. He rose a bit, enough to be able to rock back and forth, which loosened him so he could get his hands on my knees. Between the two of us, we managed to get him back up onto the island, where we both lay exhausted for several minutes.

Whistle Pig is my student. I take this role seriously as I have been mentored so well by Bald Eagle. I was thrilled to have someone to teach, especially one so keen to learn. Although he came to fly fishing late in life, in his sixties, he was an enthusiastic and quick learner. Prior to finding me, he had collected old bamboo fly rods, antique reels, and classic fly fishing books. I think that he was just waiting for me to show up to help put it all together.

That day on the Platte, we had been fishing for steelhead on one of the great feeder streams to Lake Michigan. I love salmon and steelhead fishing in the rivers of my home state. It rivals anything in the country. These anadromous fish are depleted in their native western states, due to the dams and water projects there. They were planted in the Great Lakes to replace lake trout that were decimated by lamprey. They enter streams to spawn in the spring and the fall. You won't catch fish as large as these in the Rocky Mountain states. And in the Northwest, I would venture that there are not as many as in the Great Lakes feeder streams. I once observed a car with an Oregon license plate parked at my favorite stream pullout. The driver showed and I asked him why he was fishing here. He said because the fishing was so good.

As much as I love catching these big fish, I enjoy trout fishing even more. I love the progression of hatches and the exact matching required to catch selective brook and brown trout in my home waters, centering on the Au Sable and Manistee Rivers near Grayling, Michigan. Trout in the frenzy of abundance will take nothing but the exact imitation of the insect and its stage through the progression of the hatch. It is a great challenge for the fisherman and the fly tyer to get it exactly right.

Whistle Pig once asked me how I became a fly-fisherman. This caused me to spend some time thinking about it, and this is the conclusion that I came to: Fishing is a calling, and it seems more like it chose me than I chose it. As a little tyke, I loved to fish and I especially loved to watch fish. Barefoot and summer tanned, I fished from the horizontal branches of an overhanging willow. I watched the bluegills and rock bass below take my bait. I have been hooked on sight-fishing ever since. At night when I dream, I dream of watching fish.

I can't think what it is that I love most about fishing. Maybe it's the nature experience—the gurgling of a stream rolling over rocks and gravel, tree-laden banks, and tree-shaded water. Maybe it's fooling a fish with a fly that I tied myself, then catching it with a split-cane bamboo rod that I made. I love bringing a fish to hand, looking hard at it, and taking a mental photograph of it. They are beautiful, and I like to look closely at what is typical of their species, then at their individual uniqueness. I love collecting bugs, keying them to genus and species, and tying flies to match them. Then, I love carefully placing those flies in tidy rows in fly boxes, and opening the boxes later and rearranging the contents for the umpteenth time.

The second time I saved Whistle Pig was on the North Branch of the Au Sable. The occasion was the annual stream cleanup out of Gates Au Sable Lodge. We selected the beat from Kellogg Bridge to Morley Road, then set off wading down the river with a trash bag in one hand and a spiked pole in the other. Things went well at first, where the river was wide and shallow. We collected the odd bits of trash: soda and beer cans, water bottles, a lone flip-flop, a bikini top—now that will get you thinking. As we went around a couple of tight bends, the water deepened and forced us first to one side of the river and then to the other. We were careful and waded through just fine. A half mile down and just below the first river cabin, we encountered log debris that forced us to the opposite edge. I was in the lead and passed a submerged stump with some difficulty. I looked back and warned Whistle Pig about it. He nodded, looked a bit worried, and when he tried to get too far away from the stump, he tripped on something else. I was close, moved quickly, and was able to grab the back of his wader straps where they cross. As his legs slid out into the current, I kept his head above water, but his waders filled. We clambered out onto the bank, he stripped them off, and poured the water out. It was a warm day so he amiably donned the waders again and we continued down the river.

The third time Whistle Pig flirted with drowning was also on the North Branch. We were fishing with Bald Eagle on that outing. He had worked a bit ahead of us and when we came around a big bend, somewhere below Black Hole, we found Bald Eagle out of the water and on the bank. He cautioned us to come his way and said that we had to get out of the river there, that it was too deep on the far side. I was already on the far side and didn't see any serious depth there. But Whistle Pig, heeding Bald Eagle's instructions, began working towards him and attempted to cross. The water he waded through deepened and quickened. He lost his footing on the slick rocks and began bobbing downstream in the current.

I yelled for him to hang on to his fly rod, but in his panic, he let it go. I wouldn't have normally cared so much, but it was a bamboo fly rod, the first one that he had made and under my instruction. How quick he was to let it go—oh well, I guess in the face of impending drowning it didn't seem so important to him.

About twenty feet below his involuntary swim was a log sweeper. As he floated to it, he grabbed it with both hands. The current swept his legs under and he fell into a horizontal position with only his hands, the bill of his cap, and his nose visible. Bald Eagle knew Whistle Pig was in trouble and ran along the bank to help him. Whistle Pig managed to slowly hand walk his way along the sweeper back to the bank. There, Bald Eagle got hold of the back of his collar and helped pull him out. They sat there out of breath, recovering from the incident. Whistle Pig was soaking wet and his waders comically ballooned with water and trapped air.

Meanwhile, I frantically searched for the discarded fly rod. In the shallow water on the opposite bank—yes, Bald Eagle, we could have made it through just fine—I ran down and looked in the shallows below the pool. Unable to find it there, I returned to the spot where Whistle Pig first dropped the rod and found it in about four feet of water. We fished it out by catching the fly line with the hook and line off another rod. Sadly, the tip was broken and would have to wait until winter for repair.

What do you do with a guy who has difficulty wading? Well, you put him in a boat. And you put him in a boat with the guy you trust the most. That guy would be retired fire chief Steve Taylor. Who is more trusted than a fire chief? Who can be counted on to do exactly the right thing in any emergency? Who can remain calm in the direst situation? To make Steve Taylor an even better choice, he has his own boat! It is a twenty-four-foot Au Sable riverboat that he built himself from Spanish cedar and fine, marine-grade plywood. He finished it beautifully with fiberglass and multiple coats of spar varnish. It is his pride and joy and yet he is neither afraid to fish in it, nor does he fuss about it when you are in it with him.

Steve is the most observant and knowledgeable fly-fisherman I know. He does it all: fishes and casts well, ties his own flies, makes split-bamboo fly rods and, of course, the boat. Yet, like so many competent fly-fishers, he is content to remain in the background, to quietly do his thing without seeking fanfare or recognition. If you ask for help, he is quickly there to give it yet never forces it upon you.

He knows his hatches, common and Latin names, and has a fly box filled with innovative patterns for each one of them. He was the first to introduce me to Michigan's bat fly hatch, long before it appeared in any books. He ties his own very effective pattern for the hatch and one winter sent me an unsolicited dozen in an envelope. I once asked him about fishing the hex hatch, and he explained how some of the big fish sit tight to the left bank and others to the right bank. He has a box of left leaning flies for one side of the river and another box of right leaning flies for the other! Usually, I would raise the bullshit flag at such a notion, but I've learned to trust what Steve says.

When we put Whistle Pig in Steve's boat, they got along like twins separated at birth. Steve admired Whistle Pig's ardent desire to learn and easily fell into the role as teacher. Whistle Pig loved the security of the boat and the ready knowledge of its master. They went out many times that first season and Whistle Pig's fishing knowledge and expertise dramatically improved.

After they took several trips together, I asked Steve how Whistle Pig was doing. "Great," he said. "I don't know what you were talking about. In my boat, he doesn't seem to be afraid of the water at all."

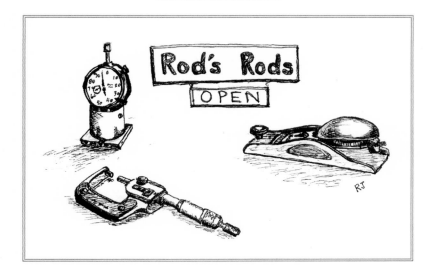

He had been silent for thirty minutes, looking out the window at the passing countryside, as I drove. Then Bald Eagle said, "That was the most fun week I've ever had!"

"Don't tell Patty that!" I advised.

"You're right … then the second most fun week," he said and grinned.

We were on our way back to the Detroit metro area, where we lived in small towns on opposite sides of the city. We had just finished the Genesis School of Rod Making and were still basking in the afterglow of a wonderful week learning the skill of split-cane bamboo rod making.

"You know, Archer, we need to make another rod as quickly as we can."

"The finish isn't even dry on the ones we just made," I objected.

"I know, but if we don't make another soon, we'll lose the skill," he said.

I knew he was right. Despite taking thorough notes and photographs, the memory of what and how we did it would soon fade. But there was another consideration, "First," I said, "we need to make the tools to make another rod." At that time, bamboo rod making was a niche craft with fewer than seven hundred devotees worldwide. You couldn't buy most of the tools necessary to make a bamboo rod; the few items that were available were of dubious quality and very expensive.

"You're right," Bald Eagle said. "Let's do that together. I don't have a workshop yet, but you do. Let's do it there."

I agreed, and we checked our calendars and found a few days, two weeks later. "We can also cast our new rods," he added. "Better hurry and wrap the guides."

In my spare time for the next two weeks, I wrapped the guides on my Genesis rod. First, I placed a spool of nylon thread on my desk and ran the free end under a heavy book. Then, twirling the rod over my lap, I wrapped the thread onto the feet of each guide. It was a slow process, but eventually I got there. After all the guides were wrapped, I applied several coats of varnish to hold them in place and make the thread lines disappear.

Finally, our workshop day came. As usual, Bald Eagle was early and excited to begin. We filled our cups with coffee and headed downstairs to my shop. He stopped in the doorway and took it all in. I had a fairly complete woodworking shop, equipped with several benches, pegboards holding hand tools, and in the center of it all was the Shopsmith that I inherited from my grandfather. This tool alone met most of my power tool needs: table saw, drill press, disc sander, jigsaw, planer, band saw, and shaper. It is amazing what Shopsmith was able to put into a tool that took up no more space than a bicycle.

The day before, I had cleaned my shop and swept it, cleared the benches, and assembled all hand tools and other items that I thought we might need.

"What should we make first?" asked Bald Eagle.

"I think we should make the tools in the order that we used them in the course," I said. "That way we could start making another rod just a step behind our tool production."

"Good idea. That would make a dull, thick-bladed knife first. That'll be easy; I just have to take one out of our kitchen knife drawer. Patty is always after me to sharpen them."

"We can procure items like that easily enough," I said.

"Yes we can, so we should make two lists: one of things that we can find or easily purchase and one of things to make," said Bald Eagle.

The list of things to purchase included a dull kitchen knife, rubber mallet, propane torch, sharpened screwdriver, flat and round wood files, vise, heat gun, hand plane, and sharpening stones.

The list of things to make included a strip holder for node work, sharpening station, beveler, Garrison binder, bamboo oven, cork press, dip tube, drying cabinet, and rod wrapper.

Two tools not included in our list were the planing form and power beveler. We had purchased the planing form that we used in class and so had in our possession the most important tool of all. The power beveler was a time-saver, but we could hand plane the initial triangle on a simple wooden form, and so we would do without the power version.

"I can set up a small workshop at home, in the mechanical room in my basement," said Bald Eagle. "There I could make some of the easier things on this list myself. So, while we're together, let's make the difficult items that will take shop tools like your table saw and drill press."

So, we decided that the best items to make together were the Garrison binder and the bamboo oven. We found plans for them in Ron Barch's *Planing Form* newsletter. We studied the plans, made a list of needed items, and then headed out to the hardware store to get them.

Parts in hand, we were ready to roll. We made our two ovens first, according to a plan by Frank Neunemann, a German rod maker. It was brilliantly simple and consisted of two sixty-inch-long aluminum stovepipes, one three inches in diameter and one five inches, and two five-inch-diameter caps for the top and bottom. The smaller pipe was fastened inside the larger, two inches above the bottom and with its top end protruding through a hole cut in the top cap. In operation, the bound bamboo strips would be lowered into the smaller pipe. The nozzle of a heat gun would be pushed through another hole in the top cap. Heat would then blow down the larger pipe, then rise up the smaller one with the bamboo strips in it. An even heat of three hundred and fifty degrees could accurately be maintained. We fastened it together with rivets and J-B Weld high-temp, metal epoxy. Next, we constructed a base of two-by-fours and plywood to stand the oven upright.

The Garrison binder was more challenging. We were not skilled at metalworking, so we substituted oak for the metal face and top plate; we crafted the center, hooked-shape holders from brass elbows. A six-foot aluminum angle bracket was fastened to the top plate and supported in-feed and outfeed arms made from PVC tubing. Spring thread tensioners and a brass guide controlled the binding thread. Small brass pulleys guided the drive belt, and a large garage door pulley with an attached handle served as the crank.

At the end of each day, we took our finished Genesis School rods out on the lawn to cast. It was a warm, sunny, late spring day, almost T-shirt weather. The snow had recently melted and the grass was starting to green.

I watched Bald Eagle cast his "Dickerson 7615." He had it down, was accurate, and laid out fifty feet of line effortlessly. Then I cast my rod for the first time and was disappointed. I couldn't make it work. It wasn't as slow as the ones at the school, but it just didn't feel right.

I handed it to Bald Eagle and asked him to give it a try. As he held it in his hands, he examined my work and complimented my guide wraps. Then he read the signature block.

"'Genesis' is a good name," he said. "I still wish I had thought of it."

"Don't forget that heart series that I suggested," I replied.

"No—too close to home. I'll stick with designer and taper. Now that we plan to make more rods, what will you call the next one?"

"I'll stay with the books of the Bible. The next will be the Exodus," I said.

Then Bald Eagle began casting my rod. He struggled with the Genesis at first but soon found the rhythm.

"This is different," he said. "You have to slow down like the others, but there is something else. It flexes deep, just above your hand and then snaps at the end. Once you load it, don't accelerate, but stop it quickly at the end of the stroke. More than the other rods, you have to let it do the work."

"Ron Barch told me that it had a 'parabolic' taper, that it flexed at the tip and butt but not in the midsection. What you are describing must be what he meant," I said.

Bald Eagle handed the rod to me. I tried to duplicate his stroke and, with some instruction from him, began making better casts. As I got the feel of it, I continued to improve.

I would cast that rod for twenty to thirty minutes every day that I was home that summer. I desperately wanted to like it ... and by the end of summer, I did. Not only could I cast it well, but I had also improved my casting ability by 200 percent. Eventually, I found that I could cast any rod better once I found its rhythm and that all rods had a rhythm.

By year's end, Bald Eagle and I not only finished procuring and making our tools, but we each made two more fly rods. The craft had us hooked, and the next year, we attended two rod-making gatherings, one in nearby Ontario and the other in Grayling, Michigan.

"Who the hell is Kastelin?" asked an elderly fellow in a Ben Hogan cap and a tweed jacket as he pulled a fly rod from the rack and read its signature.

Jim Kastelin and I were sitting on the deck nearby, eating our lunches. That remark had Jim looking up with a puzzled expression and me chuckling.

"Jim, did you put your rod in the rack with the Youngs, Dickersons, and Paynes?" I asked.

"I put it in that rack there, for all of us amateur makers," he said.

"No, that rack is in back. This rack is for the classical rods that old geezers like that guy collect. Right now, he is searching his memory bank for an antique rod maker named 'Kastelin' and coming up short. After lunch, you better move it, or you'll just confuse them all."

Jim and I, as well as Bald Eagle and some eighty other rod makers, were at Grayrock, the bamboo rod gathering held annually near Grayling, Michigan. This three-day conclave promoted the craft of split-bamboo rod making. Enthusiasts from all over the country met to discuss their pastime, conduct seminars, cast rods, exchange gear and ideas, and even fish a little. The participants were almost all old, retired, grizzled men who had enough time in their lives to devote to something as arcane as making split-bamboo fly rods.

"Gathering" was exactly the right term; like the gatherings of the old western mountain men, these were informal events of equals who loved their craft, good food, and drink. The schedule was flexible, men appeared and disappeared, and wandered about carrying fly rods, tools, and even whole culms of bamboo. At any one time, you could find them gathered in classes, or casting fly rods on the lawn, or in small groups of two or three in animated conversation. Although a few made a living from rod making, most did not, and all were eager to share what they learned from their long hours of toil and experimentation.

When Bald Eagle and I first attended Grayrock, the gathering had only been assembling for ten years. It started in 1991, on the Yellow Breeches in Pennsylvania, and moved to Grayling in 1995, where it found a home. The men we met there were some of the first to pick up the craft after its secrets were revealed by renowned rod maker, Everett Garrison, in his 1977 book, *A Master's Guide to Building a Bamboo Fly Rod.* Prior to "The Book," the few professional rod makers at the time clung to their methods with great secrecy. But the world had changed; fiberglass and graphite had replaced bamboo in the manufacturing of everyday fly rods. Those who earned a living making bamboo rods were being replaced by those who did it for the pure enjoyment of it. The time was right for a resurgence of the craft, and the book was the spark that lit the fire. The new makers, fueled by sharing and the cross-fertilization of ideas, were making better and more beautiful rods than ever before.

I can think of no other activity where two novices like Bald Eagle and me would be taken in, treated as equals, and honored for our efforts by these fine older men. In no time at all, we belonged. And, it wouldn't be many years before Bald Eagle and I would be teaching classes and devising new tools for our craft. Eventually, we would sit on the Grayrock Board that organized these events.

After my first rod that I named Genesis, I made the Exodus, Leviticus, Deuteronomy, and Lamentations. Then my enthusiasm for Bible names faded, and I looked for other ideas—perhaps too soon, because "Revelation" would have been a great name!

Eventually, I designed my own taper—designing is too strong a word— I modified the Paul Young "Martha Marie" by reducing the line weight from a six to a five, moving the action closer to the tip, and eliminating cane where it wasn't needed, making it both lighter and smoother. To make these changes, I used instructor Wayne Cattanach's "Hex-rod Program," a digital tool that was not available at the time Paul Young made his classic rods.

My new taper needed a name. So, I chose to call it and future rods after aircraft that I had flown. I knew that this was a solid, mid-weight, everyday rod, so I called it the "Phantom" after the F-4, in which I had logged more than two thousand hours of flight time. I would follow that with others. The modified Paul Young Midge became the "Tweet," and there was the "Talon," and the "Viper."

But it was the Phantom that I would make most often. As luck would have it, it turned out to be a sweet fly rod, casting near or far with pinpoint accuracy. Others asked for the taper, which I was glad to share, and soon a half dozen rod makers were producing it. Eventually, I further modified the Phantom to a seven-foot-nine-inch six-weight and a seven-foot four-weight. These three rods would all cast with the same feel and could cover a wide variety of stream conditions.

There is no real money to be made by making split-bamboo fly rods. The forty to fifty hours that go into a rod returns, if you are lucky, maybe a thousand dollars. Subtract the costs for materials and you are earning little more than minimum wage—minimum wage for a highly skilled craft. Bamboo rod making is woodworking to a machinist's standard of a thousands-of-an-inch. I know a skilled rod maker who can make more money from his wooden, hex-shaped rod tubes than he can from the rods themselves.

Jeff Wagner, an Ohio rod maker, does it all: makes fly rods, teaches weeklong classes, and sells components and tools. He once told me that you could make a small fortune in rod making ... provided you started with a large fortune.

I have enjoyed two avocations in my life: flying and rod making. And I did neither with the intent of making money. Fortunately, flying jobs paid well. Please don't tell Northwest Airlines or the union, but I would have flown for half the pay! And for rod making, the reward is the craft itself and then fishing the product.

Bald Eagle has sold a few of his rods, but I have sold none. I have not been willing to turn a fun craft into a business that entails time constraints, cost considerations, and customer demands. But, you do reach a point where you have so many bamboo fly rods that you have to do something with them; after all, a closet can only hold so many. Between Bald Eagle and me, we have given all the Venerable Fly Tyers one of our rods. It is a thrill to watch our buddies fish them, handle them so carefully, and honor them.

I have made a fly rod for each of my eight grandchildren and inscribed his or her name and birth date in the signature block. For now, at least, I've put each rod in a sock and tube and hidden it away in my gun safe. If I live long enough, I'll take each grandchild fishing on his or her sixteenth birthday and present the rod. If I don't live that long, they'll find the rods at my passing and know that I loved each so much that I made them a handcrafted heirloom.

A craft so loved requires you to put something back into it. With that in mind, Bald Eagle and I joined the Bamboo Bend Project. Bamboo Bend was started in 2012, when two Grayling fishermen put their heads together to find a program to benefit disabled veterans. They were already bringing the vets to the Au Sable to fish but wanted to do more for them. So, Victor Edwards and Jim Ottevaere came up with the idea of a bamboo rod-making school. Veterans would devote six days to rod making followed by two days of guided riverboat fishing. While Ottevaere provided most of the start-up funds, Edwards provided the facility—the garage workshop at his river home. Project Healing Waters sent the students.

Dennis Higham was drafted to run the operation and write the syllabus. Ron Barch became the lead instructor. Other instructors that first year included Peter Jones and Mike Biondo. Grayling guides quickly volunteered to take the participants fishing. And all of this was at no cost to the vets.

After two years, the school was such a success that Edwards built a pole barn in his backyard to house it, and the garage morphed into a dining hall. The program added students, eight in all, and more instructors, including Bald Eagle and me.

Many of the vets had serious physical disabilities; almost all had post-traumatic stress disorder (PTSD). The program gave them the sense of camaraderie they had enjoyed on active duty and something to do with their hands and minds. The fishing community of Grayling lavished love on them with generous financial gifts to help run the program. Folks frequently came by to drop off old fishing gear, books, and other handmade items. Some came just to watch and offer encouraging words. The Oxbow Club, a hundred-year-old gentlemen's fishing club, provided free lodging.

The vets flourished; smiles and friendships grew as the week progressed. It all went too fast, and at the program's final dinner party, they were presented with their finished fly rods. Although they had done all the work up to the final finish, varnish takes time to dry, so while they fished the last two days, bamboo elves dipped the rods in varnish and then polished them for presentation.

We have kept up with many of our vets over the years. Some went on to make more rods, one we even helped place in commercial bamboo rod making, and two others we are bringing back as instructors. The man who replaced retired Victor Edwards as president of Bamboo Bend is Mark Mackey, a retired Marine Corps lieutenant colonel, and one of our former students!

It was a late spring afternoon, and Bald Eagle, aka Rod Jenkins, and I had been working in his basement shop. Rod had just finished repairing a rod that our friend and instructor, John Long, had helped break. The story goes like this: While Rod was turning the grip in his lathe, the section that extended three feet out the other end was spinning erratically. John, seeing this, took a rag soaked in alcohol and lightly encircled the spinning end to control it. At first it worked, but it didn't take long for the friction to dry the alcohol, causing the rag to tightly clasp the blank. John let go but not before a loud bang was followed by a splintered, wildly flailing rod section. Rod quickly shut off the lathe, but the damage had been done.

Rod repaired the damaged section by inserting pins to spread the splintered bamboo, worked glue into the brake, then pulled the pins, wrapped the section with thread, and let it dry overnight.

Now, I watched as Rod removed the thread and scraped away the surface glue. He wiped and buffed it and then showed me the work. You could not tell that it had ever been broken. A ghost wrap and another dip in the varnish tube would complete the job—the job of a master rod maker.

As we left his shop that day, I looked back over my shoulder. There above the door hung the sign that Rod's daughter, Meg, had made and presented at Christmas. It said it all in just two words ... "ROD'S RODS!"

# ANOTHER ROCK IN THE LAMAR

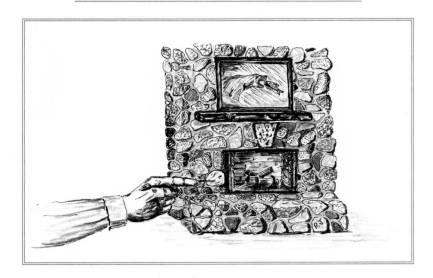

"This rock will knock 'em dead!" said Chuck as he picked up a duck-sized rock from the river's edge.

Water rolled off the glistening stone as we both examined it. "It looks like petrified wood," I said.

"You're right, Archer. And it will be the centerpiece of that new fireplace you plan to build. The one you said that you wanted to display a rock from every stream that you fished!"

"I was thinking of Michigan streams, the ones close to home, not one five miles from the car. This rock must weigh twenty-five pounds. How will I carry it?"

"You've got a backpack—put it in there," said Chuck.

I arranged my raincoat and fleece vest to cushion my back and put the rock in on the outside. It fit just fine, and when I hoisted the pack, the straps stretched a bit but held. I slid my arms through and shouldered the load. It wasn't bad … it wasn't bad at first anyway!

We had just finished our lunch break, sitting on logs below the confluence of the Lamar River and Cache Creek. Our hour-long morning hike in had us cross the creek and then fish it upstream, leapfrogging each other as we went. This is a great stream for cutthroat trout and sits well off the beaten path, ensuring little competition and angling pressure. It was a gorgeous sunny day; water glistened as it riffled between pools along rocky backdrops. The little stream was generous, giving up many fish in the ten- to fourteen-inch range. They all came from plunge pools with three to four feet of fast water before a logjam wedged into the rock behind. Large, bright, attractor fly patterns were the ticket. At one spot, Chuck took a dozen fish from a small vee formed by two logs. He thought he caught them all and moved on, but after he left, I moved in and took six more!

Eventually, we turned around and worked back downstream, passed the trail crossing, and then continued down to the Lamar. The plunge pool at the confluence held several nice fish. There I took the fish of my day, a beautiful fourteen-inch, golden Yellowstone cutthroat. I saw it rise on the far side behind a shed-sized rock. One long cast and dead drift tagged it! When the pool played out, we continued fishing down the Lamar, taking fish from all the likely spots.

At noon we stopped and ate lunch beside the river. It was there that Chuck found my heirloom rock!

As we continued working downstream, the load on my back began to wear. To make matters worse, the round rocks underfoot were covered with a thick, green layer of periphyton—rock snot to the less scientific. The footing was treacherous and I was top-heavy. If I got into any kind of rock-hopping rhythm, the pack would start to sway from side to side. The weight of the rock threw me off stride, and I would have to stop to regain my balance. After about a mile like that, we came upon an area where gas bubbled right out of the river bottom itself. Although we took a couple of fish just above, we would find no more for the next mile. The aspen and alders alongside the river were dead, and even the periphyton that had so thickly covered the rocks was gone. There was a bad odor in the air, and soon we both experienced mild headaches. Eventually, we exited this dead zone and were almost immediately into fish again.

The pack had become a real burden by the time we left the stream. We had a mile-long hike along Specimen Ridge Trail to our car parked above the footbridge across Soda Butte Creek. Chuck helped by carrying my fly rod and vest so that I could place my hands under the straps of my backpack and ease the load off my shoulders. Eventually, we reached the car and I dropped the pack like a hot potato and stood up straight for the first time in a couple of hours. We broke our rods down and inserted them into their tubes. Off came boots and waders.

After our gear was stowed, we began the forty-minute drive back to our cabin. Along the road winding through verdant valleys, we had several encounters with many of the park's animals. We stopped to watch the Druid wolf pack hunt the wide valley along Soda Butte Creek. Farther on buffalo crossed the road near the Pebble Creek campground. When the big animals are out, gawkers form and slow the transit, but on that day, we were glad to be among the onlookers.

Finally, we drove into the Silver Gate Cabins and parked. I took my rock out of the backpack and began examining it. Other members of the Venerable Fly Tyers gathered and I proudly showed it off.

Ken Miller asked, "Where did you get that?"

"Along the Lamar River," I said.

"You know it's illegal to take anything out of the park," he admonished.

Actually, I didn't know that. I knew it was illegal to deface park trees and rocks and such, but I didn't know that taking one rock was illegal.

"What if everyone took a rock out?" he continued.

"First of all, not everyone is going to haul a twenty-five-pound rock five miles for the grueling fun of it," I said. "And secondly, it seems like there are rocks all the way down to the center of the earth, so I doubt any would be missed."

"How will you take it home on the airplane?" he asked. "What if someone asks you where you got it?"

I was getting irritated now and exclaimed, "No one will ask that!"

But Ken must have gotten inside my head because I started worrying about how I was going to get the damned rock home. That is, until Mal

Canter and his party drove into the lot. He cautiously came to a stop on the gravel road and everyone bailed out. While the rest of us had rental cars, Mal had driven out to the park from Michigan, partly to make a long, scenic trip of it, but mostly because he was afraid to fly. So, I asked Mal if he would carry my rock back home in his car.

"I don't have room for it," he said.

"It's only the size of a toaster," I exclaimed.

"I don't have room for that," he insisted.

I let that sit for now, but I was surprised that he wouldn't help me out. He was a good friend and we had been generous with each other before. This seemed out of character.

Later, on the day that we packed for home, I waited until his car was loaded and then showed him where my rock would fit. Again, he claimed that he didn't have room. When I pressed him a bit, he said, "You seem like a prosecutor pushing my case hard. Okay, I don't want to take it. You took it out of the park illegally and I don't want to abet your criminal activities. Besides, what if I was stopped and asked if I had a rock in my car?"

"Does that happen to you often?" I asked.

"Ah … no. But, if it did, I am a lawyer and cannot tell a lie!"

Ken Miller, hanging on the edge of our conversation, said sarcastically, "That is exactly what people pay you to do. You lie so we don't have to!"

Mal, insulted, persisted, "I could lose my law license and be disbarred if it was proven that I lied. So again, what could I say?"

"You could say that a friend asked you to carry the rock home so he wouldn't have to take it on the airplane!"

"What if they asked where it was from?" He just wouldn't budge.

"You could, in all honesty, say it was from Wyoming!" I said.

He still refused, leaving me to take the rock home on the airplane. At that point, Chuck, seeing my frustration, said that he would carry it on the flight.

Later that day as we approached Billings's airport security, Chuck took my backpack and put it on the belt. After scanning, the TSA agent took it aside, opened it, and asked, "What is this?"

"It is a rock," Chuck said, stating the obvious.

"Yes, I see that. It's not from the park, is it?"

I was dumbfounded; maybe Mal Canter was right. But Chuck was quick. "It's from Wyoming."

"Oh, okay," said the inspector. "I just have to ask, because people are constantly trying to steal rocks from the park."

Unbelievable!

For my birthday that year, I received a package from my daughter Katie in California. It was small but very heavy. I opened it and found a yellow rock and a picture of Katie holding it in front of a rock wall with a sign above that said, "$500 FINE FOR TAKING ROCKS." Katie had heard my Yellowstone story and cleverly thought of the gift. I put Katie's rock in the basement next to the rock from the Lamar. That spring I gathered rocks from my favorite Michigan streams: the Boardman, Manistee, Pere Marquette, and all three branches of the Au Sable.

When summer came, I hired Ron Mikula, the expert mason who built Chuck's fireplace. Together we built mine. By that I mean he designed it, chose the stones, and set them, while I merely did the grunt work of mixing mortar and carrying rocks. In addition to my river rocks, we incorporated an arrowhead that I found as a child and a piece of flint from the ruins of the altar of the Abbey of Bury St. Edmunds, in England. In the year 1215, at that very altar, the Anglo-Saxon knights and nobles swore an oath to press King John to sign the Magna Carta. I had picked up that stone during my Air Force assignment to England. If I had been an astronaut and walked on the moon, somehow I would have hidden a lunar rock away in the pocket of my space suit, and it would have been built into my fireplace, too.

Perhaps I do have a problem taking rocks!

# DENNY'S WAKE

In July of that year, we lost our first member of the Venerable Fly Tyers. Denny Hanley had fished with us in May after returning to Michigan from his new home in North Carolina. Three years prior, he had taken a job in that state, found a wife, and begun a new life. We missed him at our meetings and outings and were glad for his return.

Denny was a tall, slender, red-gone-white-haired gentleman. He was quick to smile, laugh, and tell a good yarn like many of the descendants of the Emerald Isle. But he had a serious side that railed against any form of government or business red tape or nonsense and was frequently heard to say, "This is bullshit!" Because of that, the Venerable Fly Tyers used the term "bullshit" to describe any form of untruth inflicted on us versus "making up crap" for the untruth we inflicted on others.

Denny loved all forms of hunting and fishing but was particularly fond of trout and woodcock. Many a Venerable Fly Tyer eagerly accompanied him to field or stream. He was especially popular in our group and so welcomed back to our midst.

On that long weekend in May, we stayed in the rental space above The Old AuSable Fly Shop. This was once the home of the Steve Southard family who ran the shop for twenty-five years, when it was called the Fly

Factory. It slept eight and we crowded it. That week was a time of fishing, take-out dining, fly-tying, and, of course, late nights of "making up crap." Denny was the center and we orbited around him like planets unable to escape his gravity.

But something was wrong. Denny was even more ebullient, chatty, and friendly than usual. He went out of his way to connect with and compliment each of us individually. And some of us saw something that nobody mentioned at the time but we talked about later: Denny's skin was gray. Later in June, Denny revealed that he was dying ... dying from a fast-moving adrenal-gland cancer, a painless, energy-sucking, untreatable disease that took our friend in less than six weeks from diagnosis to death. The only mercy was that it was quick and he didn't have to suffer from the cut, burn, and poison standard of American cancer treatment.

In his last days, he would only take calls from two of our members, Bald Eagle and Viking. They had been closest to him. With dignity, he met his death on July 16. We mourned.

His ashes were returned to Michigan. A public funeral was held at his old church in Ann Arbor for family, friends, and associates. The church and cemetery services were packed.

But, that is not the end of Denny's story, for the Venerable Fly Tyers had something else in mind. We would hold a riverside service, in the true tradition of an Irish wake. A date was set for the next season, calendars cleared, and all fourteen members of the Tyers descended on Grayling, Michigan, on the third weekend in May.

Bald Eagle had withheld some of Denny's ashes from the Ann Arbor funeral and prepared the eulogy. On a warm, cloudy day in May, we assembled at the parking lot of Lower TU, a Trout Unlimited property in the Holy Waters about a two-hour wade above Wakeley Bridge. Two bends above the bridge was the site chosen for our ceremony. Denny, Bald Eagle, Hellman, and I had night fished the big bend pool there on several memorable occasions. Denny enjoyed taking some fine fish from those waters and once told Bald Eagle it was his favorite spot on the Au Sable.

It was about an hour's river wade, with no fishing, to the bend. As the members assembled, Moyski and I slipped upstream a couple of turns. We thought that since we were going to be on the river with fly rods, we ought to at least fish a bit, totally in the spirit of Denny, and if Denny were alive, he'd have joined us. Perhaps he did.

Eventually we caught up with the group. They had filed up the river two abreast, rods held high, sending the fishermen they encountered scurrying downstream or forcing them out of the water altogether. Moyski and I silently picked up the rear. When we came around the last bend, we saw onlookers gathered at a couple of cabin docks to honor Denny. Sensing something of import, even strangers had joined the gathering.

At this point what I am about to relate, although seeming somewhat fantastic, is the truth ... no making up crap, no bullshit. It really happened this way.

We formed up in two rows of seven apiece with about two rod lengths between us. Bald Eagle took the container of Denny's cached ashes and waded to a position at the head of the lines. Just as he was about to begin his eulogy, two kayaks came around the bend. We had the center of the river and they skillfully skirted us to one side and passed by. About to start again, Bald Eagle was interrupted when a third kayak came around the bend. In it was a middle-aged man, almost naked except for a small thong. Unskilled, he panicked and headed for the middle of the group, then at the last moment changed his mind and tried to slip around the edge. But he picked the wrong edge, where there was a large, half-submerged log, and he hit it broadside. His kayak flipped and hung inverted in the lee of the log. For a long moment, the turtled kayak was all we could see. Two of our members, Tom Roberts and Jimmy Chang, hustled through the waist-deep water and reached under and retrieved the drowning kayaker. They held his inert body up by the armpits. We all held our collective breath, until with a cough and a sputter, the kayaker came to life. Other Tyers quickly flipped the kayak, drained the water, and retrieved the paddle. Hellman set the confused soaker in it, put the paddle in his hands, and shoved him off downstream, where he quickly disappeared around the bend. Denny would have loved it!

We sent a lookout upstream to check for more kayakers, and then reformed for the ceremony. Bald Eagle began his eulogy. His kind words reflected how we all felt about Denny, how he would be sorely missed, and that he lived his life well. When Bald Eagle finished, he came to attention and commanded, "Fly Tyers, atten-hut. Present rods!"

As we came to attention and outstretched our rods to touch the tips, Bald Eagle dumped Denny's ashes in the stream. They flowed through us and down into the bend, where we hoped they would settle and rest. Then the clouds parted and a shaft of sunlight shone down on us. Two woodcocks flew upstream and one of them flew off into the woods, sort of an avian missing man formation. Somewhere, Denny smiled!

A few years before Denny's passing, Bald Eagle made a bamboo fly rod for him. It was my Phantom taper. He was presented it at the Venerable Fly Tyers Winter Party that year. Denny was grateful and made a big deal of receiving it. Afterwards, though, I don't think that he fished it much. Often the gift of a beautifully appointed split-cane rod is only lightly fished. The recipient is afraid to damage or break it; better to hang it on the wall and show it off.

After Denny's wake, his daughter returned the rod to Bald Eagle. We took it to Yellowstone that year. Our plan was that every day it would catch the most fish. Bald Eagle accomplished that on day one and Moyski on day two. Day three was my turn. At the end of the day, when the others had finished, they gathered around me and discovered that I was two fish behind. I then had several Venerable Fly Tyers trying to guide me to every visible fish in the Soda Butte. Finally, after taking three more, we quit for the day, with Denny's rod count still intact.

On day four, it was Viking's turn. Viking made no real effort to catch the most fish. We were concerned but then realized, "This was perfect!" Denny must have been looking down and saying, "This is bullshit" … because he never caught the most fish. He liked sitting on the bank, enjoying the scenery and the friendship. He tasked Viking with showing how Denny's rod should be fished. Viking enjoyed sitting on the bank of Soda Butte Creek, liked watching his friends catch fish, and even enjoyed a nap on the riverbank. Perfect: That's exactly what Denny liked!

# THOUGHTS FROM 35,000 FEET

I removed my headset, stowed it, and turned up the volume on the cockpit speaker. We had just leveled at 35,000 feet and were on autopilot. I monitored the aircraft radios and cleared the sky before me—my only tasks for the next three and a half hours. We were on our way to San Diego, heading west with the setting sun. Our climb out from Detroit had been routine. All the tasks associated with flight planning, preflight, and takeoff were literally behind us. In fact, we wouldn't get busy again until about thirty minutes before landing.

I reclined my seat a bit and looked over at the first officer. At this point, we usually begin a conversation, but he had pulled out a book on electrical engineering and had begun to look it over. Normally, we don't read in the cockpit, but I let it go—you never know when that stuff might come in handy! Besides, I wanted time to reflect on the past week.

My mind returned to Nettie Bay, Michigan, and a course I took there in split-cane bamboo rod making. At a long table in a room heated by a large stone fireplace, I was instructed in the art of splitting and planing cane. By week's end, I had taken a twelve-foot-long culm of bamboo and turned it into a six-sided rod, its action so I alive I itched to fish it. I had made graphite rods before, but this was something different—a combination of craft and art that left my mind whirring. I envisioned other rods that I wanted to make and how I could construct the jigs and machines to do it.

I also thought about how the week had become something more than making rods. It was the coming together of eight students, all good men, and two patient and caring instructors. We worked together, ate together, and talked late into the night about rod making, fly fishing, and life. The setting was scenic, the lodge comfortable, and the food outstanding. It was one of those rare and perfect weeks—measured best by how everyone lingered after the last breakfast, no one in a hurry to leave, no one wanting it to end.

A radio frequency change brought my mind back to the cockpit. Surrounding me was one of modern technology's finest machines. I scanned the eight CRTs that display flight and engine parameters. Data link connects us to our company's dispatchers, schedulers, and maintenance. We can even print out the messages. On board are over one hundred microprocessors. Not only do we fly by wire, but even the toilets flush by computer! DIGITAL with capital letters!

Although I'm comfortable with this technology, at some deeper level, I long to make fine things with my own hands. And, in my mind, I put another coat of finish on my new cane rod, and felt it warm to my touch as I rubbed the slick oil in.

The sun set as we passed over Alamosa and the San Luis Valley. Any other day, I would think of fly-fishers plying the Rio Grande here for its best trout. But today my reverie wanders to the valley's history. Like the Russian steppes, it cradled civilizations. Many cultures of Native American people prospered on its abundant game and fertile soil. Their populations grew until they overfilled the valley and moved on … it was a place of Genesis! Nettie Bay was the Genesis of my fly rod making. And I know, as certain as this setting sun, I will make many more!

# THE CABIN

"Well, here it is," said Chad. "Let's see what's wrong with it!"

Realtor Chad Brown had picked me up at my home that morning. We had driven to Grayling, all the way talking about fly fishing, rivers, and the price of frontage. Twenty minutes east of town, we crossed the Au Sable's North Branch at Kellogg Bridge. We looked at a couple of other river properties first and then finally drove to the cabin that I was interested in.

For some twenty years, I have wanted a cabin on the river but never found the right one. The stream or section wasn't right or the cabin needed too much work, and the better ones were too expensive. Two weeks before my trip with Chad, I had even decided to stop looking. I cancelled my search with both Trulia and Zillow. But Zillow didn't die easily and gave me one last intriguing lead, a cabin on the North Branch of the Au Sable completely furnished and listed well below market value. Even then, I wouldn't have made this trip ... except that my wife was visiting her sister in Oregon.

Chad and I parked under the big white pine and looked hard at the cabin. It was old, dark brown, and log sided, but it had no obvious disrepair. The roof looked solid with years left in the shingles. It sat not more than twenty-five feet from the river and on a great section of water.

Chad unlocked the door and we stepped in. We didn't take more than three steps before we stopped in our tracks and stood in wonder. It was neat as a pin, inviting, homey; the perfect fisherman's cabin. The walls and ceiling were knotty pine. Large windows, which looked out onto the river, surrounded a dining nook. An old brick fireplace adorned the opposite wall. The main room was furnished with Rittenhouse and Habitant furniture. That didn't mean much to me, but Chad knew its value and pointed it out. Two small bedrooms were equally well furnished and inviting. The beds were made, there was silverware in the kitchen drawers, and the liquor cabinet stocked. I felt like Goldilocks in the house of the Three Bears. Three twenty-plus-inch trout hung on the walls. A large sign above the entrance to the kitchen read, "Sailor's Fly Factory." In short, there was "nothing wrong" and everything right about this cabin.

After regaining our equilibrium, Chad looked at me and said, "One of us is buying this cabin today. Is it going to be you or me? You have first claim, you found it, and you are the client. But, if you don't want it, I do!"

"Chad, that's the greatest real estate sales technique that I have ever seen. But I can't buy it today; Mary has to see it first. I have an agreement with my wife that I don't buy any river cabins when she is out of town!" I said.

"We need to put an offer in today, and it has to meet their asking price. It was listed by a Bay City realtor, who obviously has no understanding of the value of Au Sable River property. It is at least 30 percent underpriced. We are the first to see this cabin and it will likely be snapped up tomorrow," he said. "How 'bout I put in the offer and give you and Mary a week to decide? No sales technique—I am hoping you won't buy it!"

Two days later, Mary returned from her trip. She handed me a four-page letter explaining why we shouldn't buy a cabin. She had stayed up all night on the red-eye scribbling her dissertation. Of course, I couldn't really disagree with anything she said but insisted on showing her the cabin "that we weren't going to buy."

The next day we drove over to the North Branch and to the cabin. Mary brought along her friend, Crystal, to support her decision. We weren't there five minutes before Crystal whispered in her ear, "I can't support a 'no-buy' decision; this is a fantastic deal."

Another five minutes and Mary was taking pictures of everything. I knew that sign. I approached her and asked, "Does this mean that you want to buy the cabin?"

"Oh yes!" she said.

I was eager to tell the Venerable Fly Tyers about my new cabin, fish that we would catch, and good times we would have. The news would lift their spirits. We had lost our first club member, Denny Hanley, to cancer earlier in the summer. We had fished with him in May, not knowing that anything was wrong, and by mid-July, he was gone. He left us sad and missing his gregarious Irish mirth and all-around good humor. He lingered on everyone's mind.

So, I decided to have some fun announcing the cabin. I had keys made, hot-melt glued them onto three-by-five cards, below which I wrote the lat-long of the cabin and nothing more. I put them in envelopes and mailed them from Grayling with no return address. Then I waited, wondering what fantasies and mental machinations would ensue.

Soon email traffic picked up from the members. Selected excerpts went like this:

*On Sep 19, at 9:35 AM, Viking wrote:*
I just went through my mail after returning from Yellowstone and found a bubble pack postmarked Grayling. After having Thor sniff it for explosives, I opened it. In it was a key attached to a piece of paper with a lat and long on it. The location is on the North Branch just south of North Down River Road. My immediate thought was that it was Denny's way of saying he had left me a cabin in his will. But I just talked to Bald Eagle and discovered that he received one also. That is strong evidence of the Denny connection. Anyone else get one?

*On Sep 20, at 9:22 AM, Bald Eagle wrote:*
Guys, the address at the lat long is, 2051 Garber Trail Rd, Grayling. This address appears to be on the north branch. Was it owned by Denny and he is willing it to the Fly Tyers? This location appears to be an access that Denny,

Nial, and I have fished a few years ago. It is also where Archer, Hellman, and I have fished.......Mmmmm, interesting.

If Doc is at his cabin maybe he can drive over and check the address. Go east on north down river rd and just past the north branch turn right on Garber Trail.

The plot thickens! After Denny's Memorial rod's performance and this new mystery, Denny's memory certainly lives on. Might be worth a road trip just to check if there is a pot at the end of the rainbow! Maybe the key unlocks something special!

Life is good! Bald Eagle

*On Sep 20, at 11:10 AM, Rusty wrote:*
I searched yesterday and a bit this morning. Nothing has come up yet using owners name of Hanley or with the address. I'll look some more later tonight. Also, I have not yet received a key in the mail. Maybe this is a plot.

*On Sep 20, at 3:39 PM, Viking wrote:*
I'm going to take the envelope to work and ask our carrier what it means when the postage is from one place and the cancellation is from another. I think I'll also fingerprint the paper, envelope and key.

*On Sep 20, at 4:40 PM, Bald Eagle wrote:*
Good idea!! This might be a case for mail fraud, maybe the FBI should be called in!!

*On Sep 21, at 7:00 AM, Moyski wrote:*
I was wondering if anyone else received the key. Hopefully some answers to follow!

Any chance this has something to do with Denny's ashes?

*On Sep 21, at 9:29 AM, Bald Eagle wrote:*
Maybe!? I got the ashes but no guidance where to put them. I was thinking of the big hole/bend upstream of Wakeley bridge road. We fished there as often as anywhere. It is just upstream of the cottage that we frequently rented with Hellman, Nial, and Archer. I can remember nights fishing there

with Hellman, Archer, and Denny. One of Denny's biggest fish that I witnessed him catching was one evening during a brown drake spinner fall. No matter the source of the mystery key, it has kept the memory of Denny alive and prominent.

*On Sep 21, at 10:25 AM, Doc Scott wrote:*
I am up at Edgewater and plan to drive over to the location mentioned in a little while, will let you know what I find.

*On Sep 21, at 12:52 PM, Chef Marquardt wrote:*
Is this some sort of Geo Cache thing that will lead us to the next Lat/Log for another mystery?

*On Sep 21, at 1:12 PM, Viking wrote:*
So has anyone other than Bald Eagle and me received a package? I've attached a scan of what I received. Now that Inspector Doc Scott is on the case I'm sure we will get some answers. The black and white panther.

*On Sep 21, at 1:50 PM, Chef Marquardt wrote:*
Here's my theory. The red stamp on the back of the envelope indicates that the envelope was purchased in Traverse City. The person then drove to Grayling to mail the keys. The fact that only two keys have surfaced so far leads me to believe that the keys open some type of pad lock that only came with two keys and the sender did not have extras made. The lock was purchased at the Do it center hardware store on M-72 in Grayling.

*On Sep 21, at 1:59 PM, Doc Scott wrote:*
Through persistent and high level investigative work, I have learned at least two vital facts regarding the mystery key. 1) the lat long coordinates are either inaccurate (which could be an additional level of devious behavior) or, the assignation of them to the 2051 Garber Trail location was inaccurate, or they were merely an approximation. In fact, DO NOT proceed to the above address as you will be met by a curmudgeon with blood shot eyes in a modified golf cart. I have certainly seen such people on the golf course, but he was definitely out of place and a bit intimidating in the Garber Trail setting. 2)

the actual location we are curious about is at 2047 Garber Trail road. It is a lovely log cabin right on the beautiful North Branch. It has what looks like a small unattached bunkhouse, and one other shed-like out building. It has many beautiful mature pines and wooden steps that lead down to the very nearby river. (see attached photos). I have also learned that its ownership has recently exchanged hands and does reside with one of our dearly beloved. However, I feel revelation of this ownership will soon come to us all from another source.

*On Sep 21, at 2:20 PM, Bald Eagle wrote:*
Thanks Doc. This is better than most mystery novels!!!! My guess it was done by colonel mustard in the library with an inheritance!!! Suspects in this order: Archer, Hellman, Chef, Doc. This is as good as any road rally/scavenger hunt that I have been involved with!! Maybe we can get to the bottom of this Wednesday night at my house! Meeting number one of this year's Venerable Fly Tyers schedule.

*On Sep 21, at 2:25 PM, Moyski wrote:*
This is quite the mystery, which makes me want to jump to the end of the story.
    This is beginning to smell like a Bald Eagle plot that involved roping a certain Archer to do the dirty work.

*On Sep 21, at 3:16 PM, Bald Eagle wrote:*
The plot thickens!!!

*On Sep 21, at 5:07 PM, Viking wrote:*
My guess: Colonel Hellman, on the North Branch, with an elk hair caddis.

*On Sep 21, at 5:21 PM, Bald Eagle wrote:*
Colonel Archer, in the den with his laptop!!! He has been way too conspicuous with his lack of response.

*On Sep 21, at 5:25 PM, Viking wrote:*
Or, Professor Archer, in the woods with a bow.

*On Sep 21, at 7:22 PM, Bald Eagle wrote:*
Guys, Viking wanted to go check out this lat long thing and go on a road trip this week with me. Sorry too busy ...... PT for knee Monday Wednesday Friday am, art class Monday afternoon, tutoring Tuesday morning, injection of synthetic chicken fat into my arthritic knee Tuesday afternoon, hosting fly-tying Wednesday night, Axel all day Thursday, airport open house Saturday with Andy and Axel, kayaking with Meg on Sunday, oh .......and just added joint replacement seminar Monday night.

*On Sep 21, at 7:54 PM, Moyski wrote:*
Mary and I are going to try and spot the place on our way up to the UP this weekend.

*On Sep 21, at 8:06 PM,* I wrote under the pseudonym *"Brown Drake":*
> Lat longs aren't just anywhere,
> They are clues for those who dare.
> Unlock the door with the key.
> Enter joyfully and see,
> What you are invited to share.

*On Sep 21, at 9:36 PM, Viking wrote:*
All I know is that I think I have a place up north...........until the locks get changed. A fishwagon on blocks as it were. Sweeeeeeeeeeeeeeeeeeeet!

*On Sep 22, at 12:50 AM, Rusty wrote:*
OK, Here are some of the things I found out. There are current listings in Trulia and Realtor.com for 2047 Garber Trail. Trulia shows it being sold on 8/28/14. The attached documents are from the Crawford County website which isn't very extensive. It shows a Parcel ID # and a pretty good idea of the location on a map. Rick, can you confirm the location from your trip there? If this property recently sold it may not be recorded yet or more appropriately not showing in the public records yet. Crawford County shows the current owner as William Peters. I'm trying to get to plot maps and the register of deeds for Crawford County charges $70 for a report. Sorry, I'm not paying that much unless I know it will be worthwhile. I've only received emails on this, no key. I'll keep looking as I have ideas.

*On Sep 22, at 5:41 AM, Viking wrote:*
Trump, you better get to bed. Bald Eagle will be knocking on your door in just a few hours ...

*On Sep 22, at 8:12 PM, Bald Eagle wrote:*
I can't make it up until next Wednesday. Sounds like a great place, Archer. Is my bamboo order there or do I still have to pick it up in traverse city? Viking, Moyski did get a key also. I think there are only four of us with keys. Archer has fished the most with the 4 of us ..... I think we are zeroing in on the mystery, another poet no less!

*On Sep 22, at 9:08 AM, I wrote:*
You have found me out! Archer

*On Sep 22, at 11:10 AM, Moyski wrote:*
This is so totally awesome! Do we need chairs and cigars too, along with some whiskey for sitting out by the river?

*On Sep 22, at 11:28 AM, I wrote:*
It came fully furnished with a full liquor stock and chairs—bring cigars!
   Archer

Shortly after the email string, Hellman was the first to arrive at the cabin. Mary and I were there cleaning the dust and debris from the long period of unoccupancy. Hellman was excited and I was thrilled to show him around. I pointed out the guest cabin, a small outbuilding with bath and bunks that can sleep four. A couple more members of the Venerable Fly Tyers came that fall. Then at the end of October, I closed the cabin for winter.

   Now that I owned a cabin on the river, I had no reason to keep the old Fishwagon. How do you sell something that you only paid one hundred dollars for and got ten thousand dollars' worth of enjoyment? So, I merely gave it away. The first responder to my ad was a certain Reverend Ragan, who showed up in an old pickup truck. He was a slight man in his seventies, disheveled, and with one wild eye. I wondered what church he was reverend of. He had two young woman with him, not overly attractive, but overly made up. We loaded the camper in the bed of his truck. As I watched the reverend and his entourage drive away, memories of the Fishwagon flooded my mind and emotions. I don't know what use the reverend had in mind for the Fishwagon—he was evasive when I asked—but the feeling I got was a bit on the sketchy side. I hate to think of it being idle; perhaps it has found good use as a homeless shelter or in the Detroit sex trade!

In early May of the next year, the cabin hosted the Venerable Fly Tyers' Season Opener and two weeks later a dinner after Denny's wake. That was the first time that all members of the Fly Tyers got to visit the cabin. I hung all their pictures, framed in a five-by-seven format, in a large square on the wall. Another "improvement" that I added was a sign made of pine and routed with the words: HQ FOR MAKING UP CRAP. The Venerable Fly Tyers had found a river home.

# GRAMPY'S CABIN

I approached the bridge over the North Branch, slowed, checked the rear-view mirror, and came to a stop in the center of the span. I craned my neck to see upstream and then down. The water was high and colored with runoff. In-stream islands, fish structures built in the 1930s by the Civilian Conservation Corps, just barely held their heads above water. Small black stoneflies, the season's first hatch, sputtered off.

A quarter mile on, I turned right onto the first two-track. Sunlight dappled through the overhead branches as I put the old pickup truck into four-wheel drive and eased down the lane. It slipped a bit on soft clay wet with spring melt. A doe bolted across the trail not twenty yards ahead and ran into the dewy meadow to my right. She loped another fifty yards, then stopped and looked back at me. I came upon the fork and took the right branch. I had to stop twice to pull downed tree limbs out of the road. Another quarter mile and the light of the clearing revealed an old, log-sided cabin nestled close to the stream.

As I approached the cabin, the two-track gave way to grass and circled under a tall white pine, one of the first to take hold after the logging of the 1870s.

I only had two days to open and prepare the cabin for the Venerable

Fly Tyers' first trip of the season—the much-anticipated "Opener." Yet I lingered in my truck, taking in the cabin and recalling the first time that I saw it.

During the past winter, I visited the cabin once or twice a month. Although I have had it for several years now, the first moments of my arrival continue to thrill me. The minute I unlock the front door and step inside, I take a deep breath and relish the cabin's scent, best described as a mixture of aged varnish, wood ash from the fireplace, and decades-old, fabric-covered furniture. Sunlight floods through the large dining nook windows and reflects off the knotty pine walls. I walk close and look out at the river. It is usually low in winter, with shelf ice clinging to the edges. Twice in recent years it has completely frozen bank to bank—a rare event, locals tell me.

I close the cabin for winter by turning off the heat and water. But for a short stay, I can quickly warm it by firing up the propane wall heater and kindling a fire in the fireplace. I then haul water from the artesian well that bubbles out of a ground pipe not thirty feet from the door, enough for cooking and washing up.

A cabin, like any dwelling, takes on the feel and aura of those who inhabited it over the years. You can sense the difference between one that was a place of happiness from one of sadness. My cabin has the feel of good times, happy people, and sharing. It is a good and uplifting feeling. I am here alone this time but sense the presence of family and friends. I look at the wall that holds the pictures of the Venerable Fly Tyers. To one side is Denny with a black ribbon taped in the upper left corner, and I know others will follow in just a few years.

My cabin sits on a half-acre lot that was once part of the Kellogg homestead. Ed and his wife, Bessie, arrived in Crawford County in 1903 and purchased several forty-acre parcels along the North Branch from the State of Michigan. Ed was a true frontiersman and could do it all. He felled the timber and hand hewed the logs to build a large cabin to raise their growing family—a family that would eventually number seventeen children. He also built the first bridge across the river that bears his name and an in-stream water wheel to grind flour, saw lumber, and provide electrical power. Their old homestead still stands, remains in the Kellogg family, and is my neighbor to the north.

To the south and downstream is the cabin named the Goat's Nest. It sits on a half-acre lot sold by the Kelloggs in 1912 to William Miller and three other men. According to local legend, this property wasn't so much sold as lost in a poker game. Supporting that argument is the fact that the deed granted fishing rights through all Kellogg land. Ed Kellogg built the small log cabin that sits on the site, and the property is still in the hands of a relative of Miller's cousin, Sam Morley.

The next property downstream is another former Kellogg parcel. In 1918, Ed sold it to his friend and fishing companion, Guy Garber. Kellogg built the Whippoorwill, a large, two-story log cabin on the property to pay … you guessed it … a poker debt. When the cabin was complete, Garber asked Ed what he would have charged had it not been a debt payment. Kellogg said, "Twelve hundred dollars." Garber promptly paid his friend that amount.

My property was the last in line to be sold. Alonzo Collen, a descendant of one of Crawford County's earliest settlers, purchased it in 1929. The next year, Collen built my log-sided cabin. Then in 1946, he sold it to William "Sailor Bill" Huddleston, an early Grayling fly tyer, fly shop owner, and fishing legend. Sailor Bill twice won the *Field & Stream* magazine's award for North America's largest brook trout. In 1948, Sailor Bill sold the cabin to Clive and Velda Marshall, a couple from England. Sailor Bill left the "Sailor's Fly Factory" sign from his Grayling shop hanging over the kitchen entrance. The Marshalls held the property for the next forty-three years. They built the guesthouse, added on to the cabin, and lived in it year-round. Clive was an accomplished fly-fisherman and caught, from the cabin's waters, the three large brown trout that hang on the wall. After Clive passed in 1991, Velda sold the cabin to Bill and Judy Peters. Judy tastefully decorated it with Rittenhouse and Habitant furniture, while Bill stocked the liquor cabinet. After Judy died, the cabin was used infrequently. Bill eventually remarried and moved south. In September of 2014, he sold the cabin to me! No … it wasn't inherited from Denny Hanley despite the Venerable Fly Tyer legend.

The Fly Tyers quickly put the cabin to regular use. We have an annual "Season Opener" week. Then the cabin hosts the instructors of Bamboo Bend, several of them members of the Venerable Fly Tyers. The first of June, it's brown drakes, the best hatch on the cabin's waters. The third week of June is Grayrock, the bamboo rod gathering in nearby Lovells, and the time of the fabled hex hatch. The end of July, it's the trico hatch. There is grouse hunting in September and October. My son-in-law, DJ Shook, and I use the cabin as our headquarters during rifle deer season in November. We have hung and dressed numerous deer from the cabin ladder leaned against the old white pine.

My family loves the cabin, too. Mary enjoys kayaking and we host frequent summer trips with friends. There isn't a prettier stretch of river in Michigan than the ten miles of water that runs down to my cabin. All the land along the stream there belongs to the state or to large private holdings. There are very few cabins to break the spell of a wild, scenic river flowing through an ancient Michigan white pine and cedar forest.

My four daughters and their families come to the cabin every summer to canoe, kayak, swim off the dock, and lightly fish around the edges. In the evening, we sit around the fire pit roasting marshmallows and making s'mores.

One summer, we stayed in the cabin while Kristen, DJ, and their kids stayed in the guesthouse. We had ninety-five-degree days and spent most of our waking hours in the river. Cora, Margo, and Solly jumped in the river off our dock and floated the current down to the next dock, where we waiting adults helped them get out. Then they ran back to our dock, jumped in and did it again, and again, and again.

Cora is learning to fly-fish in the cabin waters. Margo loves lying on the dock and patiently netting small trout and dace in the shadows. Solly is permanently clad in a life jacket and bears constant watching, as he can't help jumping in the river every chance he gets.

We've collected monarch caterpillars from streamside milkweed plants. We took them home and watched them pupate, later emerge as butterflies, and inhabit our backyard flower gardens.

When Carrie and Joe bring their three, Caspian and Torin play "skinny sumo wrestlers" on the dock in their underpants. They lock arms and shoulders and see who can throw the other into the water. Nava says that she can just sit in a chair and watch the river flow by all day.

Katie and Derek's Miles and Graham love swimming, canoeing, and finding frogs, turtles, and snakes along the river's edge.

One day Mary told me that we should give the cabin a name and hang a sign over the door. I realized then that I wanted my cabin to be a legacy for my daughters' families and their children, my eight grandchildren, who are well on the way to building cabin memories. It also must be there for the Venerable Fly Tyers until their last day. I plan to structure the ownership so that happens and bequeath money to pay taxes, insurance, and upkeep for many years after my cabin picture, too, has a black ribbon in the corner.

I once read a Gordon MacQuarrie story about a man who spent an entire summer on the banks of Wisconsin's Brule River. He went there broken and in despair and, after that summer, had been healed by old "Doc Brule." I can picture someday, long after I am gone, one of my grandchildren perhaps unemployed, or recently divorced, or in general despair, with no idea of what to do or where to go. I hope that then he or she thinks of the cabin and memories of childhood happiness and good times. I want him or her to be able to come and spend a healing summer at "Grampy's Cabin!"

# RIVER TIME

Astoryteller's best friend is time: the time when we fished the Au Sable or the Yellowstone, the time when we drank to your health, the time we talked until two in the morning, the time that she entered my life, the time we loved, the time she left, the time we buried Denny. A story is a journey back in time. It happened, we can't change how it happened, but we can live it again in memory.

Of the four dimensions in our lives, time is the one that is the most difficult to wrap our minds around. It's been said that time exists so all things don't happen at once. Yet the pace of time is not uniform. It slows to a crawl when we are waiting. When we are absorbed in play or work, it races. It can only be stopped when we are lost in the moment.

When we are still, there is a patina to the present moment, a warm glow of being. Living in the present moment is to live in the quiet space between past and future, the stillness of now, to merely unfold on the journey of awakening.

When we are active, there is an edge to the present moment and living in it is like a surfer riding a great wave. There is only the edge of the wave— no past, no future—just now. We think the wave is water, but it is not water. There would be water without the wave, and then there would be no surfer's ride. The wave is energy and the water only the medium. The energy is the energy of creation, the energy that has surged through the cosmos since the moment of the big bang. By living in the present moment, we ride the wave of creation.

When I am on the river, I am in deep time, river time—time when living in the moment lingers into one long, slow moment. Time when I think of no other thing than fishing. Time when I think of no other time than now. Yes, only here and now, and never-ending—that is river time.

# ABOUT THE AUTHOR

Dave Jankowski is a retired U. S. Air Force fighter pilot and Northwest Airlines captain. He is an ardent fly-fisherman, fly tyer, and bamboo rod maker. With a passion for veterans, he participates in Project Healing Waters Fly Fishing and its affiliate, Bamboo Bend, where he serves as lead instructor. He lives in Traverse City, Michigan, with his wife, Mary. They enjoy a long marriage, have four grown daughters, and eight grandchildren who all love to go to "Grampy's Cabin" on Michigan's famed Au Sable River.

# ABOUT THE ARTIST

Rod Jenkins, aka Bald Eagle, is a retired airline pilot and former Air Force pilot. He has witnessed many of the stories in this book and been a character in a few.

In retirement he has pursued his interest in art: Watercolor painting and drawing have been his main interests.

Rod has enjoyed all things fly fishing for more than 50 years. He enjoys fly-tying, bamboo rod making, and time spent sharing these skills with anyone interested. One of his greatest joys is being an instructor in the Project Healing Waters/Bamboo Bend School that teaches military veterans how to make a bamboo fly rod.

Rod resides in Southeast Michigan with his wife of 47 years. Living nearby are his two children and three grandchildren. Rod's "main mission" today is to spend time with his family, making memories that will be part of stories for years to come.

# GRATITUDE

I once read a synopsis of Larry McMurtry's *Lonesome Dove,* stating that it was a story about friendship. *The Venerable Fly Tyers* is also a story of friendship. And, to all those friends, I want to express my deepest gratitude. I have always placed the highest value on friendship, and I think because of that, I have enjoyed many wonderful friends.

So to all the Venerable Fly Tyers who have come and gone through the years and through my stories, thank you for filling my life with joy and friendship: Rod "Bald Eagle" Jenkins, Dave "Hellman," Craig "Viking" Swenson, Gary "Moyski," Rick "Doc" Scott, Tim Tobias, Gary "Chef" Marquardt, Tom Roberts, Nial Raaen, Rusty Kalmbach, Denny Hanley, Dean "Mettam," Mike "Hrabonz," Tom Means, Ron Elzerman, Ken Miller, Will Avril, Bill Stryker, Duane Creviston, Rod "Whistle Pig" Rebant, Chuck Anderson, Dan "Ducker" Flick, and Dan "Woody" Woodbury, Mike Wills, Bob Delanoy, Bill Evans and Jody Byland.

In addition, I would like to thank the good people at Mission Point Press, in particular my editor, Heather Shaw, who worked diligently and patiently to help a first-time author through the process of taking a raw manuscript to the printed book that I am proud to put my name on. Also, I would like to thank author extraordinaire Jerry Dennis for helping me become a better writer.

Made in United States
North Haven, CT
06 November 2022

26358476R00126